REHEARSAL FOR
MURDER

A Full-Length Play

Adapted By
D.D. BROOKE

From The Teleplay
By
LEVINSON & LINK

THE DRAMATIC PUBLISHING COMPANY

*** NOTICE ***

REHEARSAL FOR MURDER

A Full-Length Play

for Seven to Nine Men, Six Women

CHARACTERS

ALEX DENNISON . . . . a playwright
ERNIE . . . . the stage doorman
SALLY BEAN . . . . Alex's secretary
MONICA WELLES . . . . a star
LORETTA. . . . . .the stage manager
LLOYD ANDREWS. .the director
BELLA LAMB . . . . the producer
KAREN DANIELS . . . . an actress
DAVID MATHEWS. . . . . an actor
LEO GIBBS . . . . an actor

MALE POLICE OFFICER
FEMALE POLICE OFFICER
MAN IN THE AUDITORIUM
MR. SANTORO
SECOND MAN IN THE AUDITORIUM

Time: The present.

PLACE: The stage of a Broadway theatre.

Note: The parts of Ernie, the Second Man, the Male Police Officer, and Santoro may easily be doubled.

ACT ONE

SCENE: When the audience enters the theatre, the curtain is
up. The stage is bare except for a work light RC, which is
lit, and an old stool DL. When it is time for the play to begin,
the houselights and the work light dim out together. After a
few seconds of darkness, the work light blares on again, full
force. ALEX DENNISON enters from the back of the auditorium. He is an attractive man, intelligent, forceful, charming,
witty and sophisticated. Beautifully dressed in a sports jacket,
slacks, shirt and tie, he carries a smart attaché case. He walks
briskly down the aisle and up a few steps to the stage. He
places his attaché case on the stool DL and looks speculatively
out into the theatre. Satisfied that he is alone, he looks at his
watch, opens his attaché case, removes a pistol and opens it,
checking that it is loaded. He puts the pistol in his jacket pocket and looks at the work light.

ALEX (muttering). Lights . . . (He looks off R and L. He sees
the light board and exits L. We hear the sound of switches
being pulled on. The houselights come on.)

(ALEX looks on from L.)

ALEX. That's not it. (He disappears again. The stage lights
come on, the houselights go off and the work light goes off.

(ALEX returns.)

ALEX (self-satisfied). Pretty good. And I don't even have a union card.

ERNIE (offstage R). Who's there? Who's out there?

(ERNIE, in work clothes, enters R and squints into the glare.)

ERNIE. That you, Mr. Dennison?

ALEX. Hello, Ernie. How have you been?

ERNIE. Fine, sir. Just fine. Any trouble getting in?

ALEX. No problem.

ERNIE. Gotta be careful when the theatre's closed. Some of those junkies and winos from Broadway . . . they try to bed down in the lobby overnight.

ALEX. Encourage them, Ernie. The theatre was meant for the common man.

ERNIE. It's nice to see you, Mr. Dennison. Been a while. Nobody seemed to know where you were.

ALEX. I've been in Maine. To a little house in the woods. Took a little time to think things out. (He changes the subject.) Do you think you could find me a table and some chairs?

ERNIE. Sure. What are you having? A rehearsal?

ALEX. Only a reading. I started writing a new play.

ERNIE. That's where it all begins, right? With the words?

ALEX. Yes. With the words.

(SALLY BEAN, a very young, bright but naive girl, enters from the rear of the auditorium. She seems very innocent among the sophisticated theatre people who will come. At the moment, she is rather nervous. She carries a large manilla envelope.)

SALLY (calling). Mr. Dennison! Mr. Dennison?

ALEX. Yes, Sally.

SALLY (running down the aisle). Oh, thank heaven it's the right place. It was all so dark and spooky out there. I thought a real, legitimate theatre would be all lit up.

ALEX. Not when it's closed, dear.

SALLY. Oh, yes. Well. I suppose that's right.

ALEX. This is my new secretary, Ernie. Sally Bean, all the way from Maine.

SALLY (climbing onto the stage). I've never been in New York before. I mean, doesn't it make you nervous?

ERNIE. No.

ALEX. You got the scripts?

SALLY. Yes. I went to the duplicating place and I told them to put it on your bill and then I walked left to Broadway, then right for seven blocks, then right again and I'm here.

ALEX. No trouble?

SALLY. Well, a funny-looking man in a big hat and high-heel shoes asked me to have breakfast with him but I just said it's after one o'clock and I've eaten lunch and then I walked very fast.

ALEX. Terrific, Sally. You have proved you can handle the big city. Now, will you take the scripts out of that envelope and put them on my attaché case . . . (He points to the stool DL.) . . . over there?

SALLY. Yes, sir. (She takes the scripts and places them on the attaché case.)

ALEX. The chairs, Ernie.

ERNIE. Oh, yeah. (He starts off L, then turns back.) Mr. Dennison, I . . . I never got to talk to you at the funeral . . . but I wanted you to know how sorry I was.

ALEX. That's very kind of you.

ERNIE. Seems like such a long time ago. But it's only a year, isn't it?

ALEX. Yes. A year. Exactly. One year. (A pause.)

ERNIE (not knowing what else to say). I'll get the chairs. (He goes off L. ALEX stands looking out at the theatre, then he speaks to SALLY.)

ALEX. You know, you're right. There is something spooky about an empty theatre.

SALLY (nodding after ERNIE). What he said . . . he meant about Miss Welles, didn't he?

ALEX (surprised). You knew about Monica?

SALLY. She was a big movie star, Mr. Dennison. The last few years we've had movies *and* newspapers in Maine.

ALEX. I didn't mean that the way it sounded. I meant, you knew about Monica and me?

SALLLY (nodding affirmatively as she moves DL). Was this the theatre?

ALEX. Yes. (As ALEX speaks the stage lights dim and he is picked up in a follow spot.) This theatre. A year ago tonight. It was all brightly lit . . . the marquee lights twinkling . . . you could feel the electricity of a Broadway opening night in the air.

LORETTA (offstage, over the intercom). Ladies and gentlemen, the call is half hour to curtain . . . half hour.

ALEX (walking slowly DR, the spot following). Half hour to curtain. The theatre isn't open yet but the first few audience members are waiting in the lobby . . . the people that sit in the balcony . . . they get in early to watch the celebrities come in. Backstage is a mass of flowers . . . telegrams . . . little gifts the cast exchanges with clammy hands. I got out of my cab in the fifties. I was too nervous to sit still. I walked the rest of the way. I went down the little alley and into the stage door. (He exits DR.)

(The spot holds. ERNIE appears in it from DR.)

ERNIE. Good luck, Mr. Dennison. Hope it's another one like *Laughter in the Dark*. (He exits. SALLY exits with the stool and attaché case.)

(ALEX reappears in the spot. He has exchanged his sports jacket for a dark jacket that matches his pants. A rolled-up newspaper sticks out of his jacket pocket. He stands DR.)

ALEX. I came through the wings to the stage heading for Monica's dressing room to wish her good luck. I was surprised to see her standing on the stage. (The spot goes out as the stage lights come up. The curtain now covers roughly two-thirds of the stage.)

(MONICA WELLES stands LC looking out front. A beautiful woman in a smart dressing gown, her makeup is on but she still has a few curlers in her hair. ALEX moves to her.)

ALEX. Monica! Why aren't you in your dressing room?
MONICA (nervously). I'm almost ready. I just couldn't stand it in there alone anymore.
ALEX (amused, but sympathetic). My poor darling.
MONICA. I just thought if I could come out here and get the feel of the theatre . . . before there was anyone in it . . . that maybe I could cope with it later when it was full.
ALEX. It's just opening night jitters.
MONICA (with amused sarcasm). Oh, is that what it is? I thought maybe it was just garden-variety sea sickness . . . like the people on the Titanic had when the band played *Nearer My God to Thee*. (ALEX laughs.) Alex! What if I don't remember the lines? I know I won't remember the lines. I'll go blank the second I walk onstage.
ALEX (amused). You'll be marvelous.

MONICA. They'll laugh at me.

ALEX. They're supposed to. It's a comedy.

MONICA. Who invented opening nights? This is barbaric. (She extends her hand.) Look at that! I'm actually trembling. I never get this way when I'm doing a film.

ALEX. I've told you. Movies are for children. The theatre's a different animal.

MONICA. As long as it doesn't bite. Oh, Alex, I want to be good. I want to make you proud of me.

ALEX (embracing MONICA). You will. (He prepares to kiss MONICA.)

MONICA. Don't! I love you, but it took me half an hour to get my lips on right. (She hugs ALEX. Her hand touches the newspaper and she pulls it out of the pocket.) Oh, you saw this.

ALEX (nodding). I'm sure everyone did. Nobody dares miss Meg Jones' column.

MONICA. At least we don't have to keep secrets anymore. (She reads from the paper.) "Cat out of the bag department. Actress Monica Welles and playwright Alex Dennison have a major announcement to make tonight."

ALEX. She makes it sound like we're taking back the Panama Canal.

MONICA. "The couple's hush-hush romance during rehearsals for the new Broadway comedy *Chamber Music* finales in a quiet wedding tomorrow whether the play is a hit or a flop tonight. Congratulations, fellas, and sorry to spoil the surprise."

ALEX. Has a certain way with words, doesn't she?

MONICA. I'd like to wring her neck. How did she know?

ALEX. We took out a license and we got ourselves a judge. Somebody has a big mouth.

MONICA. And Meg Jones has two big ears. If I ever run into

her . . .

ALEX. You'll be perfectly charming. Gossips gossip. That's
their job.

(LORETTA, an efficient-looking woman, comes on DR carrying
some telegrams.)

LORETTA. There's some more wires, Miss Welles. (She hands
the telegrams to MONICA.)

MONICA. Thanks, Loretta. (She hands LORETTA the newspaper.) Here. Put this in the kitty box, will you?

LORETTA. Shouldn't you be combing out? It's fifteen minutes
to curtain. (She exits L.)

MONICA (aghast). Oh, Lord! I'm still in my curlers. When I was
a little girl, I was going to be a nurse. Where did I go wrong?

ALEX. I think I'll leave before you break out in hives. (He
starts to exit L.)

MONICA. Alex? (ALEX stops and turns around.) I'm scared
to death.

ALEX (moving back to MONICA and taking her hand). If it
helps, I love you.

MONICA. That helps. Oh, the hell with my lipstick! (She
kisses ALEX.) That's it. No more butterflies. I'm going to be
wonderful.

ALEX. I never doubted it.

MONICA (taking a step L, then turning back). Alex . . . foolish
question . . .

ALEX. Mmm?

MONICA. You have a lot of . . . power. I mean, people in the
theatre will do pretty much what you say. Isn't that right?

ALEX. So I keep telling them. But if you're asking me to bribe
the critics . . .

MONICA. Nothing like that. But I suppose you could keep

someone from working if you wanted to.

ALEX. Probably. If I was vindictive instead of the tender-hearted creature you've come to adore. What's this all about? Someone put pepper in your face powder?

MONICA. Just wondering.

ALEX. Monica, you're serious. Why?

MONICA (touching her hair and feeling the curlers). Oh, Lord. The curlers! Did I tell my dresser to iron the second act costume? Alex, I've got to go. (She runs DL, pauses, then turns.) I love you . . . and . . . what do you say in the legitimate theatre? Break a leg! (She runs off. ALEX looks after her, puzzled.)

(LLOYD ANDREWS enters DR. A good-looking young man with a brisk, capable manner, he is dressed in a dark suit, with shirt and tie, and carries a clipboard.)

LLOYD. Ten minutes to blast off. I've given my last note. How's Monica?

ALEX. Traditional response. She's terrified.

LLOYD. I just talked to our leading man. David's making room on his shelf for a Tony.

ALEX. Good. Let him keep thinking he's the star.

LLOYD. Well, I hope they all do justice to the words.

ALEX. Lloyd, it's a nice little commercial comedy. Nothing cosmic. If we're a hit, fine. If not, we'll survive.

LLOYD. Either way, I'm grateful for the shot at directing it.

ALEX. Don't get maudlin on me. You did a good job.

LORETTA (offstage, over the intercom). Ladies and gentlemen, two minutes. The call is two minutes. Places, please.

LLOYD. Well, that's it. (He starts off R, then turns back.) Where are you going to watch? Back of the house or from the wings?

ALEX. Watch? You've got to be kidding. That's cruel and
unusual punishment. (LLOYD exits R. The stage lights black
out as ALEX is caught in a spotlight.) You see, Sally, I can't
sit still and watch my own opening nights. It's too nerve-
wracking. Those months . . . sometimes years of work . . .
and if the critic has a stomach ache . . . or a fight with his
wife before the show . . . if he doesn't find it funny, or
dramatic, or whatever . . . all that work is gone. So I wander.
Backstage. Outside. Front of the house. Gentlemen's lounge.
That night, I waited backstage till the house was dark, then I
sneaked up the stairs and, when the curtain went up, I peeked
through the curtain of the front box. The set looked nice.
The actors knew the first ten lines of dialogue. I went down
to the lobby . . . talked to the doorman . . . then, when I
couldn't stand it anymore, I went inside. Bella Lamb, the
producer, was standing in the back.

(BELLA comes into Alex's spotlight, looking straight ahead at
the show. Elegant and expensively dressed in furs, jewels and
a long gown, she is a stew of nerves.)

BELLA. Women should never be producers.
ALEX. Is it your nerves?
BELLA. My feet. Men producers can stand in the back and they
don't have to wear high heels. (BELLA exits.)
ALEX. I went out again . . . down the street to a little coffee
shop called Nora's. The coffee's rotten but you can always get
a table. I talked to Nora. I had coffee. It tasted like Swiss
cheese. I came back. I sat in the men's lounge where I could
hear the dialogue, whatever laughs there were. Suddenly, I saw
Lloyd.

(LLOYD comes into Alex's spotlight, looking green.)

ALEX. How's it going? (LLOYD signals his inability to speak. About to be sick, he rushes off.) Lloyd was in no condition to tell me. I went back outside. I was in front of the stage door when the first act broke and Loretta, the stage manager, came out for some air.

(LORETTA comes into Alex's spotlight.)

LORETTA. Alex! How can you be out here when everyone else is in there watching your baby being delivered?

ALEX. I'm trying to forget. How did the first act go? Don't tell me.

LORETTA. Went very well. A lot of laughs.

ALEX. I didn't hear that. (LORETTA exits.) I walked around the block. When I got back, most of the audience had gone back in for the second act but Bella was still in the lobby.

(BELLA comes into Alex's spotlight.)

BELLA. Come and watch, Alex. I'm gambling six hundred thousand dollars on this show and the least you could do is watch the opening.

ALEX. I gambled two years' work, Bella. I'm taking the night off.

BELLA. Speaking of gambling, what's this I read about you and Monica in Meg Jones' column. Is it true?

ALEX. Would Meg Jones lie?

BELLA. Amazing. I've been at every rehearsal but I never knew you two were even . . . even . . .

ALEX. Keeping company? We were discreet. Didn't want to upset any apple carts. We were going to announce it at the party tonight.

BELLA. Then that's why Monica wanted to give the party at her apartment?

ALEX. Right. You'll be there?

BELLA. Of course. (A buzzer sounds.) Oh! Oh! It's act two. (She raises her eyes to heaven.) Oh, God, let them laugh at that business with the champagne bucket. (She rushes off.)

ALEX. I walked around the block again. And again. Eight times. Maybe twelve. I don't know. Even the panhandlers stopped asking me for money. The last time, when I got back, the critics were just rushing out to make their deadlines. I tried, as usual, to read their expressions. Pleased? Annoyed? They all looked like they had nothing on their minds but getting a cab. Inside the theatre, the cast were taking their bows.

(A special light comes up DL where KAREN DANIELS, a pretty young girl wearing a coat and carrying a purse, is bowing. We hear applause.)

ALEX. Karen Daniels . . . she had a small part in the second act and understudied Monica . . .

(LEO GIBBS, a chunky, balding, character comedian wearing a raincoat, joins KAREN in the light.)

ALEX. Leo Gibbs, the comic, and then . . . our leading man . . .

(DAVID MATHEWS, tall, handsome and a little smug, joins KAREN and LEO. Dressed in a host jacket, he bows grandly.)

ALEX. The ever-popular David Mathews . . .

(BELLA comes into Alex's spotlight and applauds madly.)

BELLA. Nice of you to drop by.

(MONICA joins the OTHERS in the bow light. The applause becomes louder. ALEX applauds.)

BELLA (to ALEX). Now you applaud! Where were you when we needed laughs in the scene with Karen? (She exits. ALL but MONICA leave the bow light. MONICA bows again. The applause becomes louder.)

ALEX. The audience loved Monica. I could tell that. Whether or not they liked the play, I didn't know. But they loved her. And she was radiant. (The bow light goes out. The applause stops. MONICA exits.) Monica didn't even change. She left the theatre immediately. She was giving the party and she wanted to get out before those hordes of phony well-wishers stormed backstage. In five minutes, backstage was a zoo, a jungle. The publicity man had a national magazine he insisted I talk to, so by the time I got to Monica's the party was in full swing. (The sounds of a tinkling piano and party conversation come up and play behind the following.) It looked like the zoo had been moved from the theatre to Monica's living room. I didn't see Monica. The actors were by the food. Naturally.

(KAREN, in a pretty party dress and carrying a plate of food, comes into Alex's spotlight. She appears rather innocent and very excited.)

KAREN. Isn't this wonderful? I keep bumping into famous people.

ALEX. They're rented for the evening. And they'll all disappear if the reviews are negative.

KAREN. Oh, but we're going to be a hit. The audience loved it.

ALEX. You're new to the theatre, Karen. First lesson is never to confuse the audience with the critics.

KAREN. When will we hear about the reviews?

ALEX. Someone will phone them in to Bella.

KAREN. Oh, that's why she's in the kitchen.

ALEX. The kitchen?

KAREN. By the phone. With Lloyd. They're just standing there staring at the phone. All evening. They didn't even eat. (Reminding herself, she begins to eat.)

ALEX. The death watch. It's better on an empty stomach.

(DAVID MATHEWS, carrying a plate of food, and LEO GIBBS, carrying two glasses of champagne, enter Alex's spotlight. BOTH are dressed in dark suits.)

DAVID. Where's Monica? The hostess should put in an appearance.

LEO. I guess she wants to make an entrance.

DAVID. Obviously. But it's a bit overdue.

ALEX. I'll go and get her.

KAREN (nodding behind her). I think that's the bedroom.

ALEX. No, dear, it's the study. The bedroom is beyond it. (To LEO, indicating the champagne.) Let me take those, Leo? Monica may need some. (LEO hands the glasses to ALEX. At the same time, the curtain behind them opens to reveal Monica's study. *See Production Notes for set description.* DAVID, LEO and KAREN exit L to the party. The stage lights come up on the study and Alex's spotlight goes out. The party noises go down, but continue as from L. ALEX moves to the door UR and calls.) Monica! Monica?

MONICA (offstage R). That you, Alex?

ALEX. Yes. Come on out.

MONICA (offstage R). Give me a minute.

ALEX. The natives are getting restless. They want to see the hostess.

MONICA (offstage R). Coming . . .

(MONICA enters UR, through the door. Dressed in a glamorous hostess ensemble, she carries a manilla envelope. She crosses to ALEX and kisses him lightly on the cheek.)

MONICA. Darling . . .

ALEX (offering MONICA champagne). Need some wine?

MONICA (smiling). Yes . . . in a minute . . . Put them down there, will you? (She nods to an upstage table, then moves to the sofa and sits.)

ALEX (putting the glasses on the table). What were you doing?

MONICA. The truth? I was standing on the terrace, outside the bedroom, looking over the tops of all the buildings all the way back to Broadway and all those lights.

ALEX. Standing on the terrace?

MONICA. Thinking.

ALEX. But it's beginning to rain.

MONICA. Did my hair come down?

ALEX. You look beautiful.

MONICA (nodding "thank you," then opening the envelope, withdrawing a stack of bills, and counting). I'll just be a minute.

ALEX. Well, I've seen actors do strange things after an opening night, but counting money?

MONICA. I got this from the bank today. Would you believe it? With all the excitement, I ran out of cash. (She puts the money back into the envelope and holds it out to ALEX.) Put this somewhere for me, will you, darling? I don't like it lying around. (ALEX takes the envelope and moves to the desk. He pauses at the sound of distant thunder.)

ALEX. Thunder. Signs and portents. Let's hope it's not an omen. (He opens the top left desk drawer and reacts in amusement.) What's all this?

MONICA (laughing). That's my junk heap. There are still things you don't know about me. (Incredulous, ALEX takes out a round piece of glass and holds it up questioningly.) It's a monocle. Doesn't everybody have one? (ALEX holds up a small knife.) Girl scout knife. An heirloom. (ALEX takes out a flashlight.) Oh, well, that's a necessity. I bought it this morning. There was a power failure last night. No lights for nearly two hours.

ALEX (shrugging, smiling and putting the objects and the envelope of money in the drawer). Living with you is going to be an adventure. (He shuts the drawer.) Which reminds me, the sooner you go out there and face the mob, the sooner we can get them out of here. We've hardly had a moment alone for days.

MONICA. Alex, I'm getting married tomorrow.

ALEX. I know. So am I.

MONICA. In Judge Ebersole's chambers?

ALEX (faking surprise). Why, yes!

MONICA. What a coincidence! Noon?

ALEX. Actually, yes, it is noon.

MONICA. Oh, what good luck! I must be marrying you! But since I am, you see, I'll need all the time I can get tonight to get myself together . . . to get ready. So when I get the troops out, I'd like to be alone tonight.

ALEX (seriously). Really?

MONICA. Well, you shouldn't see the bride before the wedding. Do you mind?

ALEX. A little.

MONICA. I'll make it up to you, I promise. (She rises and kisses ALEX.)

ALEX. That's a good start. (He takes Monica's hand and leads her to the door UL.) Now, you go in there and show 'em what a real star looks like. (He drops Monica's hand and gestures for her to go.)

MONICA. Come with me?

ALEX. I'm only the writer. Stars make entrances alone.
  (MONICA blows him a kiss, then goes off L. He watches
  proudly as we hear a round of applause and cries of "Monica!"
  "You were wonderful!" "What a performance!" "You've got
  the Tony all sewed up!" etc. The party sounds die down a bit,
  but continue. He walks back to the desk, reopens the drawer,
  looks at the mess again and laughs.)

(BELLA enters UL. ALEX hears her and slams the drawer shut.)

BELLA. I couldn't get near the bar. I seemed to remember
  Monica kept a tray of spirits in here.

ALEX. You don't drink.

BELLA. That was yesterday.

ALEX. Have you had a phone call?

BELLA. Three.

(LLOYD enters with two drinks.)

LLOYD. Here, Bella, I knocked over the costume designer and
  got through to the bartender. (He hands BELLA a drink.)

ALEX. Were they that bad?

BELLA. Bad is a relative term. (She takes a gulp.) As a matter
  of fact, the reviews were mixed. Some were good, some were
  bad. But I think the *New York Times* sent an obituary writer.

ALEX. That's the regular critic. They say he eats his young.

BELLA. And, if the *Times* is bad, it hardly matters what the
  rest are. Sorry, Alex.

ALEX. What did they say about Monica?

BELLA. They liked her. Nothing ecstatic. The *Post* thought she
  was a little stiff.

ALEX. I don't want her to see that review.

LLOYD. Can't we try for a run? Her name means something. So does yours, Alex.

ALEX. It's up to the producer. (He walks to the window and stands with his back to BELLA and LLOYD.)

BELLA (setting her glass down). Let me sleep on it. That is, assuming I can sleep. I'll see the ad agency tomorrow and assess the damage.

LLOYD. If we could just stay open for a few weeks, get some word of mouth . . .

BELLA. We'll see.

ALEX (looking out the window as thunder rumbles and the party noises fade out). There it is . . . the storm. It's starting to come down in buckets. (He turns back to BELLA and LLOYD.) Appropriate, don't you think?

BELLA (going to ALEX). There, there, Alex. We tried our best. We really did. (She kisses ALEX on the cheek and starts for the door L.) It's the nature of the beast . . . and there's no beastliness like show beastliness.

(KAREN enters L, cutting off Bella's exit.)

KAREN. Oh, are you leaving, Mrs. Lamb?

BELLA. I thought it was time. The coach turned back to a pumpkin.

KAREN (unsure what BELLA means). Oh. Well. Good night.

BELLA. Don't be silly. (KAREN steps aside and BELLA exits.)

KAREN (to ALEX). You were right. I never saw people leave a party so quickly.

ALEX. Departing the sinking ship. How are you? Bearing up?

KAREN. I don't know. It hasn't hit me yet.

(LEO bustles in and goes to ALEX.)

LEO. Alex, I don't care about the reviews. I think it's a terrific play.

ALEX. Thanks, Leo. That's just what I wanted to hear.

(MONICA enters L. ALL turn to her.)

MONICA. I never saw anything like it. Nobody read the reviews but they all seemed to know. The pianist stopped playing in mid-bar. There's nobody left but the caterers.

ALEX (moving to MONICA). I'm sorry.

MONICA. Don't be.

ALEX. You're amazing. I've had a few hits so I can be philosophical. (He admits that it's not true.) More or less. But it's your first time out. You're being very stiff-upper-lip.

MONICA. Oh, I wanted a success. But I care more about the playwright than the play.

ALEX (touched and smiling). And my daddy told me never to marry an actress. (He kisses MONICA.)

(DAVID MATHEWS enters, his hair and face wet, coat collar turned up.)

DAVID. Oh, sorry, Monica. I just wondered if I could borrow an umbrella. It hasn't rained like this since John Huston filmed the Noah's ark sequence.

KAREN. Can't you get a cab?

DAVID. There's one parked across the street but, naturally, the idiot's got his off-duty sign on. That's what I love about New York.

LEO. On the other hand, if we were doing a movie in California, there'd probably be an earthquake.

MONICA (laughing). Sorry, David, I loaned Bella the last umbrella.

DAVID. When your luck goes, it goes. Well, after those notices, maybe I can use a cold shower. Good night, again.

KAREN. Leo and I are coming, too. Maybe, if it's three against one, we can frighten a cabbie into taking us.

DAVID. We can try. Come on. (He exits L.)

KAREN (to MONICA and ALEX). I'm awfully sorry. See you at the theatre tomorrow.

LEO (staunchly). I still love it. (He and KAREN exit L.)

ALEX. Sure you want me to leave?

MONICA. Of course I don't want you to leave.

ALEX. Then . . .

MONICA. But you have to. An actress has to prepare herself, so does a wife. I'm going to make myself a pot of tea and go to bed and drink it.

ALEX (reluctantly). All right. Call you at ten in the morning and wake you up. Will that give you enough time to get to the judge's by noon?

MONICA (nodding, as ALEX moves to the door UL). Alex? (ALEX stops and turns back to MONICA.) You do love me?

ALEX. Very much. Why?

MONICA. I was such an idiot last week.

ALEX. Past history. You were angry.

MONICA. Not much of an excuse. Missing a performance, stranding everybody. And that isn't even the worst part.

ALEX. Monica, is something wrong?

MONICA. Not if you love me. (ALEX finds this a curious remark and stares at MONICA. There is a clap of thunder and the stage blacks out. MONICA exits in the darkness. At the same moment, a spot picks up ALEX who continues to stare at the place where MONICA just stood.)

ALEX (completing the memory in his head). Get some rest,

darling. (He walks downstage, the spot following him. The curtains close on the study behind him. He speaks as he walks slowly DR.) I had to walk home. The rain was torrential, the wind whipping it in sheets along the cross streets. It was a little more than a mile to my apartment house. When I was about half a block away, I did see an empty cab. He even slowed down as though to entice me. I guess I was the only passenger walking around New York that late at night. By the time I got up to my apartment, I could hear the phone ringing from the corridor. (He exits DR. The spot holds. There is the sound of a phone ringing. He speaks from offstage.) Hold it! . . . Wait a minute! . . . (A thump.) Damn!

(ALEX reappears in the spot DR, wearing a wet raincoat, holding the telephone and rubbing his leg.)

ALEX. Hello?

MONICA (offstage, on filter). Alex?

ALEX. Monica . . . I just got home. Let me get my coat off.

MONICA (offstage, on filter). Alex, I know how awful it is out, but . . . can you possibly come back here?

ALEX. What? When?

MONICA (offstage, on filter). Right now. Alex, I'm sorry, but . . . please. It's terribly important.

ALEX. I thought you wanted to be alone?

MONICA (offstage, on filter). I did, but— (A loud click of disconnection cuts MONICA off.)

ALEX. Monica? Monica! (He clicks the telephone bar.) Hello? (He pushes the cutoff bar down again, then dials Monica's number. The phone rings and rings but she doesn't answer. He places the phone off behind the proscenium, then walks slowly C in the spot as he talks.) By the time I got back, there must've been five police cars in front of the building. And an ambulance. They were just lifting one of those stretcher things

into it. Whoever . . . whatever was on it, was completely
covered. I tried to get through . . . tried to see . . .
they . . . the cops . . . wouldn't let me. They told me to go
up to the apartment. There was a crowd in the lobby . . .
neighbors . . . I don't know . . . some in robes . . . some
in raincoats. An old man with a little dog. When I got up to
the apartment, the door was open. The janitor was there . . .
a police officer . . . a woman. I told her who I was and she
took me into the study. (The curtain opens on the study and
lights begin to come up on it. ALEX walks to the door UL and
his spot dims as the other lights come up.) The living room was
still a mess. Somehow the caterers hadn't cleaned up after the
party. There was another policeman sitting at the desk in the
study. He was on the phone.

(The lights are up on the study. A male POLICE OFFICER is on
the phone. ALEX stands a little right of the doorway. A
female POLICE OFFICER stands behind him in the doorway.)

MALE OFFICER (into the phone, not seeing ALEX). Welles,
Monica. That's right. Of course, she was dead when we got
here. It's a ten-story drop. (ALEX groans. The MALE OF-
FICER looks over at him.)
FEMALE OFFICER (to ALEX). Perhaps we'd better wait in
the living room. (ALEX shakes his head, moves to the chair L
and sits. To the MALE OFFICER.) This is Mr. Dennison, Miss
Welles' fiance.
MALE OFFICER (to ALEX). Oh, I'm sorry, sir. (ALEX nods.
The FEMALE OFFICER moves to the table UC and pours a
drink. Into the phone.) No, her fiance just came in. (To
ALEX.) How did you happen to come by, sir?
ALEX. She called me.
MALE OFFICER. How long ago?
ALEX. Half-hour . . . forty minutes. I couldn't get a damned

cab! (The FEMALE OFFICER brings ALEX a drink.)

FEMALE OFFICER. Here. Take this.

ALEX. No, thank you.

FEMALE OFFICER. Better have it, sir. You've had quite a shock. (She hands the glass to ALEX. ALEX raises it to his lips, then lowers it.)

ALEX. I really don't want it. (He turns to put the glass on the table beside him and sees a small tray with a pot of tea, a cup, saucer and sugar bowl.) She always made herself a pot of tea before she went to bed. She . . . (He suddenly puts the glass down, stands and turns away from the OTHERS. He tries to get control of himself.)

MALE OFFICER (into the phone, trying not to be heard by ALEX). She called him thirty or forty minutes ago. Okay, I'll talk to him, call you back. (He hangs up the phone, rises, moves C and looks at Alex's back. He "looks" a question to the FEMALE OFFICER who shrugs in response, then looks at ALEX again.) Mr. Dennison? Mr. Dennison?

ALEX (turning to face the OTHERS). Yes?

MALE OFFICER. Miss Welles gave a party tonight, sir? (ALEX nods.) And you were here?

ALEX. Yes.

MALE OFFICER. How was she when you left her?

ALEX (distractedly). What?

MALE OFFICER. I was wondering if she was depressed.

FEMALE OFFICER. Listen, maybe you should do this tomorrow. Talk to Lieutenant McElroy, then . . .

ALEX. No, I'm all right. No. She was not depressed.

MALE OFFICER. I guess you were the last person to see her alive.

ALEX. The caterer's people were still here when I left. They were cleaning up.

FEMALE OFFICER. They didn't do much of a job.

MALE OFFICER. Do you know any reason why . . . (He finds the question awkward and stops.)

ALEX. Why what?

MALE OFFICER. Why Miss Welles might have wanted to take her own life?

ALEX (shocked). No! No! No reason! No! I know of no reason . . . I do not believe Monica Welles would have killed herself.

FEMALE OFFICER (gently). She left a note.

ALEX. A note? No. That's not possible.

FEMALE OFFICER. It's in the typewriter.

ALEX. Typewriter? (The FEMALE OFFICER nods toward the desk. ALEX moves toward it but stops half-way.) Would you mind . . . could you read it to me?

MALE OFFICER (looking at the typewriter). It says, "I'm sorry but it's better this way." (There is a blackout. The OFFICERS exit. A spot hits the typewriter, the note still in it, and holds for a second. Then the spot blacks out and the curtain closes in front of the study. When the stage lights come up again, the curtain is entirely closed and ALEX, in his original sports jacket, stands DR.)

(SALLY sits on the stool DL with the attaché case and scripts beside her on the floor.)

SALLY. A year ago. Golly, how awful for you.

ALEX. I'm sorry, Sally, I . . . I shouldn't have burdened you with all that. It's just I've been thinking about it a lot . . . and being back here . . .

SALLY. That's all right. I mean, if it helps to talk about it . . .

ALEX. I don't know if it helps, Sally. Maybe today will help.

SALLY. You miss her a lot, don't you?

ALEX. Yes, I . . . (He is unable to speak for a moment. Not

wanting the conversation to continue, he reaches for his wallet and takes out a bill.) Sally, do something for me.

SALLY. Sure.

ALEX. Go out the stage door . . . (He points off R.) . . . turn left and go down about a half a block. There's a little luncheonette . . . sign says "Nora's." Get me about a dozen coffees, cream on the side and a dozen Danish.

SALLY. Danish?

ALEX. That's New York for sweet roll.

SALLY. Isn't that odd? (She takes the money from ALEX.) Left, half a block, Nora's.

ALEX. You got it. (SALLY exits DR.)

(ERNIE enters from C of the curtain.)

ERNIE. I set up some chairs and a table behind the traveler, Mr. Dennison. (He indicates that he means the curtain.) I think it's enough but there's more in the wings if you need 'em.

ALEX. Thanks.

ERNIE. Want me to open the curtain?

ALEX. Don't bother, Ernie. I'll do it later. As a matter of fact, why don't you take the rest of the day off?

ERNIE (surprised). Really? Well, I don't know. If anything should happen . . .

ALEX. Like what, Ernie? Plague? Pestilence? Trust me. If I smell smoke, I'll send for the marines.

ERNIE. But . . .

ALEX (putting an arm around Ernie's shoulders and maneuvering ERNIE DR). Go home. Open a beer and soak your feet. I'll take full responsibility.

(A door opens in the back of the auditorium and a MAN enters. ERNIE peers out into the auditorium.)

ERNIE (jumpy). Somebody just came in.

ALEX. First arrival. You go out by the stage door.

ERNIE. Well . . .

ALEX. Leave your number on the bulletin board. I'll call you to lock up. (ERNIE feels a little guilty but is not unhappy with the day off. He exits DR. ALEX walks DC, staring out, then calls.) Who's there?

MAN (from the back). Me. You want me up on the stage?

ALEX. No. Stay somewhere in the back where you won't be noticed. When the others get here, I don't want them to see you.

MAN (from the back). Right. Unless anyone tries to leave, then I come down and talk to them.

ALEX. That's it. It's essential that they stay here. *All* of them. If even one of them walks out, it won't work.

MAN (from the back). It may not work anyway.

ALEX. What makes you say that?

MAN (from the back). I don't know. Like I told you before, Mr. Dennison, it's your show. I'm just here to watch. (He turns and walks off to the side, out of sight of the auditorium entrance.)

(SALLY enters DR with two large paper bags.)

SALLY. I found it. That Nora is nice. She's like a real person. Not like a New Yorker at all.

ALEX. Thank you. But I wouldn't say that in public, Sally. There are about eight million people who might resent it.

SALLY. Can I put these down? The coffee one's hot.

ALEX (holding the curtain open for SALLY). Back there. Ernie put up a table. Take them out and make them look as good as you can.

SALLY. Sure will. I used to get A's in Home Ec.

ALEX. Sally, when the others come, I want this to run as smoothly as possible. You understand what I told you about setting up the scenes?

SALLY. Uh, huh.

ALEX. Ernie left more chairs out there. (He nods L.) Use them.

SALLY. Right. (She goes behind the curtain.)

(KAREN enters the auditorium. She walks down the aisle, smartly dressed, more confident than when we saw her before. She calls.)

KAREN. Alex? Hello, Alex.

ALEX. Karen, my love. Come here and let me get a good look at you.

KAREN (coming up onto the stage). I want you to know I got up at the crack of noon today. Just for you. (She hugs ALEX affectionately and he steps back to look at her.)

ALEX. You've changed. Much more . . . provocative.

KAREN. It's my new image. I got tired of being a sweet, little ingenue. Now, I'm going to be a sexy leading lady.

ALEX. Is the image working?

KAREN. I'll know in a week. I'm up for the lead in a new play. It's between me and one other girl. (She corrects herself.) Woman.

ALEX. Good luck.

KAREN. I think I'll steal one of her pictures and stick pins in it. (She laughs.) Well, why not? After all, you always said I was ambitious.

ALEX. So I did. How's Leo?

KAREN (staring at ALEX for a beat, then speaking nonchalantly). How would I know?

ALEX (embarrassed). Ooops. I forgot my own rule. Never ask

for anyone's husband if you've been away longer than three months.

KAREN. Yes. Things do change.

ALEX. I'm sorry. (She shrugs.) He'll be here today. Is that going to be a problem?

KAREN. Not at all. If I don't look down, I probably won't even notice him.

ALEX (changing the subject). Can I give you some coffee?

KAREN (looking around). Keep it in your pocket?

ALEX (going off L). No. I was just going to unveil it. (He exits. The curtain opens. The study has been replaced by six, ill-assorted folding chairs arranged in an arc RC facing facing LC.)

(SALLY is setting out the coffee and Danish on a tacky rehearsal table.)

KAREN (surprised by SALLY). Oh. Who are you?

SALLY. I'm Sally Bean. Mr. Dennison's new secretary. From Maine.

KAREN. Really? I didn't know they had secretaries there.

(BELLA and LLOYD enter from the rear of the auditorium.)

BELLA (calling as she and LLOYD come down the aisle). Hello? Anybody home?

(ALEX enters L.)

ALEX. Who's that?

BELLA. Just Jack and Jill tumbling down your little hill, Alex. We bumped into each other outside.

LLOYD. It was fate. She was getting out of her thirty-thousand-dollar limo and I was getting out of my hundred-thousand-dollar bus.

BELLA. Is that Karen?

KAREN. Hello, Mrs. Lamb. How are you? Hi, Lloyd.

LLOYD. What is this? "Remembrance of Things Past?"

ALEX. Reunions are good for the soul. Come on up.

BELLA (going onto the stage). I really hate this place. Too many memories. Alex, it's only because of my affection for you that I'm under this roof again.

ALEX. Noted and appreciated. (BELLA kisses ALEX.)

BELLA. It's been a long time. How are you, darling? Writing, I hope? (LLOYD walks onto the stage, spots the scripts and walks over to them.)

ALEX. Off and on.

LLOYD. Looks like mostly on. I see scripts. (He reaches for one.)

ALEX. Mustn't touch! Not yet! We still have to wait for the rest of the cast.

KAREN. Cast?

BELLA. He's being mysterious. It's the playwright's prerogative. And it's the producer's prerogative to have a Danish. (She walks to the table. The phone rings off R.)

KAREN. What an odd sound. Someone calling an empty theatre.

ALEX. Will you get it, Sally? Near the stage door.

(As SALLY starts R, ERNIE appears R.)

ERNIE. There's a call for you, Mr. Dennison.

ALEX (annoyed). Ernie! I thought you went home.

ERNIE. I didn't feel right about leaving, Mr. Dennison.

ALEX. Take the phone, Sally. (Angrily, to ERNIE.) I told you it wasn't necessary to stay.

ERNIE. I mean, it's my job to look after the place.

ALEX (in a burst of temper). Ernie, I don't want you here! Is that clear enough?

ERNIE. But . . .

ALEX. Go home. You're not needed.

ERNIE (surprised by Alex's intensity, backing off). Okay, Mr. Dennison. Sure. Whatever you say.

ALEX (embarrassed by his outburst). Sorry, Ernie. I don't know what's the matter with me today. (He walks ERNIE off, handing him money.) Here. Take this for your trouble.

ERNIE (slipping the money in his pocket). Oh, I can't do that, Mr. Dennison.

ALEX. Forget it. I'll call you when we're finished. (ERNIE exits.)

(As ERNIE leaves, he crosses SALLY who is returning DR. The OTHERS go to the coffee table.)

SALLY (to ALEX). It's a Mr. Santoro . . . (ALEX gestures for her to lower her voice. She continues to converse with him, unheard.)

LLOYD (at the table UC). Alex seems jumpy today. Not at all like him.

KAREN. Wouldn't you be? This theatre . . .

BELLA. And you realize it was exactly a year ago that . . . that the play opened.

KAREN. I didn't think of that.

BELLA (sipping coffee). I'd swear this coffee comes from Nora's. She makes the only coffee I've ever had that tastes like tuna fish.

(LEO GIBBS enters unnoticed from the back of the auditorium and makes his way quietly to the foot of the stage before ALEX.)

ALEX (to SALLY). Tell him to make it as fast as he can. He can park the truck in the alley by the stage door. (SALLY nods and goes off.)

LEO. There you are, Alex. They said you disappeared.

ALEX (turning to LEO). No, Leo. Welcome.

LEO. To what?

BELLA. That's a good question.

LEO. I know. It's all a plan to get me and Karen back together.

KAREN. Don't be ridiculous.

LEO. Nobody told me you were going to be here.

KAREN. Does that mean you wouldn't have come?

LEO. Hey, Alex wants me here. That's good enough for me.

KAREN. You're being obsequious, Leo.

LEO. Okay, I'll stop . . . if you'll tell me what it means. (KAREN turns away in disgust. LEO comes onto the stage. BELLA looks at her watch.)

BELLA. Alex, darling, whatever you have in mind, shouldn't we get started?

LLOYD. Still one more to come, right? Unless I miss my guess, it's . . .

(DAVID MATHEWS enters from the back of the auditorium and starts down the aisle.)

LLOYD. Speak of the devil!

DAVID. Sorry I'm late. Somebody parked a car in the middle of forty-sixth street and just went home. (He pauses in the aisle and looks at the stage.) Lord, it's a rogue's gallery up there! Are we having a class reunion?

LEO. Don't knock it. The man's passing out free food.

ALEX. Get some coffee, David, and we'll begin. Would you all take seats and make yourself comfortable? (KAREN sits in the chair furthest R. BELLA sits beside KAREN. LLOYD

sits beside BELLA. LEO gets coffee and DAVID comes onto
the stage and joins LEO at the table.)

(SALLY enters DR near ALEX.)

SALLY. No problem. They'll be here in half an hour.

ALEX. Fine. Will you give them each one of the folders and
then go set up for the first scene?

SALLY. Sure. Is this what it's really like in show business?

ALEX. Nothing is what it's really like in show business. (SALLY
nods and crosses the stage to the pile of scripts. She passes
out the scripts to KAREN, BELLA and LLOYD as the dialogue
continues. She leaves two on chairs for LEO and DAVID.)

DAVID (still at the table). Leo, old friend, didn't you once tell
me you went to medical school?

LEO. You mean before I went wrong and became an actor?
Yeah. Why?

DAVID. Because I have the king of all hangovers. What do you
prescribe?

LEO. You're just dehydrated. Have some water.

DAVID. Only if it's a good year. (He looks at the table.) There
isn't any. Coffee will have to do. (He sips some coffee.)
Comes from Nora's.

BELLA. Tuna fish taste?

DAVID. No. This one is more like Western omelet.

ALEX. Will you two join the party? (LEO and DAVID sit
down. SALLY exits L.)

BELLA. All right, Alex, you have the floor.

ALEX (DR). I want to thank you all for coming. I'm very
grateful. I know I haven't been in touch during the past year,
but I'm sure you understand it was a difficult time for me.

BELLA. Where were you? I tried to call.

ALEX. I rented a house in the Maine woods and brooded. Six months, I didn't look at a typewriter. The problem, naturally, was guilt. Guilt because I failed all of you . . . but, mostly, guilt over Monica's death.

KAREN. Alex, it wasn't your fault.

ALEX. She was depending on me to give her a success. She needed one. When it didn't happen, she went into a depression and . . .

LLOYD. Look, we all felt a little guilty. But no one could have predicted that kind of reaction. It was so extreme.

ALEX (pulling himself together). Anyway, that's over and done with. (He walks LC with determination and then faces the OTHERS.) The point is that I finally started a new play.

DAVID. Bravo!

ALEX. It's just bits and pieces, but it's taking shape.

BELLA. So that's why we're here.

ALEX. I want to try it out, see how it looks on its feet. And, naturally, I want your input.

DAVID. Why us?

ALEX. Call it making amends. I've written a part for several of you.

LEO. This is beginning to sound interesting.

ALEX. Lloyd, I'd like you to direct. And Bella, my sweet, you have first option . . . assuming you like it.

BELLA. Of course, I'll like it.

ALEX. I've rented the theatre for the afternoon. So let's read some of the scenes, talk about it and see what we've got. Oh, and by the way, it's something new for me . . . a mystery.

BELLA. Good! They do well. And, if not, you can always sell them to television.

ALEX. Unusual form. You take the audience by the hand and lead them in the wrong direction. They trust you and you betray them. All in the name of surprise.

DAVID. Sort of turns us into chess pieces, doesn't it?

ALEX. And that bothers you, David?

DAVID. In a way. The characters are always cardboard. I like roles with flesh and blood.

ALEX. I don't know about the flesh, David . . . but I can guarantee the blood.

KAREN. What's it called?

ALEX. *Killing Jessica.* (He goes to his attaché case and takes his script from it. The OTHERS react in surprise to the title. He calls off.) Sally! (He nods.)

(During the following, SALLY enters with two folding chairs and sets them RC together.)

KAREN. I like the title. Is Jessica the lead? Who plays her? Since I seem to be the only actress here . . .

ALEX (moving to KAREN). The part of Jessica is not exactly cast. But I have another part in mind for you, Karen.

KAREN (disappointed). Oh?

ALEX. Don't worry. It's a good part. You'll have fun with it. (He moves behind the chairs.)

LLOYD (flipping through his folder). Alex, these are unconnected scenes.

ALEX. As I said, Lloyd, bits and pieces. That's why I need help.

LLOYD. Can you give us an overview?

ALEX. It's a play about another play. One that's in rehearsal. (SALLY goes off L.)

KAREN. And Jessica?

ALEX (moving C but watching the OTHERS carefully as he speaks). She's the star. A rather complex character. She made several films . . . mostly fluff . . . and she was embarrassed by them. So she walked away. She hibernated, she travelled . . . then she decided to take a chance on the theatre. She got the leading role in a Broadway production, moved to New York, and committed herself to a new career.

BELLA. She sounds . . . familiar.

ALEX. Does she? Well, I always start from what I know.

(SALLY enters with another chair.)

KAREN. Alex, this character . . . Jessica. If we can believe your title, someone . . . kills her?

ALEX. Oh, yes. It's made to look like something else, but it's a murder. (SALLY drops the third chair beside the first two with a clatter. The OTHERS jump.) David, mind reading a scene?

DAVID (rising). Why not?

ALEX. You play the leading man. Handsome, attractive to women.

DAVID (laughing). Type casting.

ALEX. Sally, go over to the light board, pull number three and number seven. (SALLY nods and exits L.) This takes place in the middle of the first act. The setting is your apartment. (He indicates the three chairs.) That's a sofa.

DAVID. Am I married?

ALEX. Several times. Not currently. (The stage lights go out. Lights hit the area LC where SALLY placed the chairs. This is the playing area for the "play within the play.") You've invited Jessica over for a private rehearsal. You've told her it's common practice in the theatre.

DAVID (joining ALEX in the light, carrying his script). And she believed me?

ALEX. She must've because she comes.

DAVID. If Karen isn't going to play the part, who do I read with?

ALEX. Me, I'm afraid. (He opens the script he carries.)

DAVID. You?

ALEX. You're in the imagination business, David. Give it a

try. If it helps, why don't you think of . . . oh, Monica playing the title role?

DAVID. Monica?

ALEX. Actually, it's not a bad idea. Just pretend I'm Monica.

DAVID. But . . .

ALEX. Let's get started. At curtain, the doorbell rings. You're
offstage. (DAVID backs out of the light to DL. ALEX moves
out of the light ULC.) It rings again. You enter. (DAVID
moves into the light, past the "sofa," and reads from the
script.)

DAVID. Coming . . . just a second.

ALEX. You reach the door. Open it. (DAVID mimes opening
the imaginary door at the UR edge of the light.) Just think of
Monica. She says, "Hi. Am I early or late?"

(MONICA steps into the light in the role of Jessica. Dressed
simply, she carries a purse and script.)

MONICA. Hi. Am I early or late?

DAVID. Right on time. Come in. (He steps back toward the
"sofa" and drops his script and continues as if from memory.)
Sorry about not doing this at your place, but I'm a bit under
the weather.

MONICA. If you'd rather wait . . .

DAVID. No, this is too important. We have to protect ourselves.

MONICA. I hope that's an exaggeration.

DAVID. My dear, the director isn't up there with egg on his face.
We are. And when something isn't working . . .

MONICA (ruefully). Like act two, scene one . . .

DAVID (nodding). Among other pitfalls . . . it's up to us to
provide corrective surgery.

MONICA. Shouldn't we have told him we're rehearsing?

DAVID. Why? He's the problem, not the cure. Drink?

MONICA. No thanks. (She sits and opens her script.) I'm having trouble with some of the transitions.

DAVID (sitting next to MONICA, his arm resting behind her on the "sofa"). You have a genuine sense of dedication. It's refreshing.

MONICA. Well . . . thank you.

DAVID. That's why I'm glad we have this chance to get to know each other better. Strangely enough, it can help with the performance. (He inches closer to MONICA. She understands what he's doing and gets uncomfortable.) I suppose that's why so many leading men and leading ladies establish a very close . . . rapport. What do you think?

MONICA. I think we should work on the scene. Really.

DAVID. There's plenty of time. (He puts his arm around MONICA, then touches her ear with his lips. MONICA stiffens.)

MONICA. Please . . . I . . . we're supposed to be rehearsing.

DAVID. Are we? (He touches Monica's arm. MONICA rises abruptly.)

MONICA. This wasn't a good idea. I think I'd better leave.

DAVID (rising and blocking Monica's way). Why all the fuss? It's perfectly natural. We work together every day. We play love scenes . . . (He embraces MONICA.)

MONICA. Let go of me. Please! (DAVID persists. She pulls away and slaps him.)

DAVID. What the hell was that for?

MONICA. Just leave me alone! (She turns toward the door. DAVID grabs her arm.)

DAVID. Listen, lady, slaps in the face went out with the bustle. You agreed to come here. I didn't force you.

MONICA. Okay, I was naive. I actually thought we were going to rehearse. Now, may I go home? (She tries to pull her arm away. DAVID tightens his grasp.) Now, look . . .

DAVID. I don't like being turned down.

MONICA. And I don't like someone forcing his attentions on me. Especially someone egocentric, unattractive and a bit too old for me. (That's too much for DAVID and he slaps her.) Now we're even. I hope that makes you feel better. Good night. (She pulls her arm away, turns, walks out of the light and off.)

ALEX (from the darkness, echoing MONICA). Makes you feel better. Good night.

DAVID (alone in the light). Alex, I'm sorry but I just don't like it.

ALEX (walking into the light, script in hand). Why is that, David?

DAVID. Well, first, the part is much too old for me. And then, the man is totally unsympathetic. I certainly wouldn't come on like that.

ALEX. How would you come on?

DAVID (laughing). Privileged information.

ALEX. No, I'm serious. Let's say, just for the sake of argument, you wanted to come on to . . . I don't know . . . Monica.

DAVID. Monica? Why do you keep mentioning Monica?

ALEX. She was one of your leading ladies . . . and you do have a certain reputation . . .

DAVID. Alex, what is this? Monica and I were friends, co-workers.

ALEX. Rehearsals can be an intimate process. I got the impression you were attracted to her.

DAVID. You were wrong.

ALEX. If you say so. But it's academic, isn't it? We're talking about the scene and I thought you were excellent, David. Very convincing. (He calls.) Lights! (The stage lights come up as before. The lights on the play area go out. To the OTHERS.) Any comments? (ALL look at each other nervously.) Don't be shy.

LLOYD. Question. What are you going for? What's the point of the scene?

ALEX. The point, Lloyd, is that in a mystery everyone has to have a motive.

LEO. You mean he kills her because she turns him down?

ALEX. I didn't say he's the culprit, Leo. But vanity can be a powerful force.

DAVID. Nobody will believe it. You don't commit a murder just because someone rejects you.

ALEX. No? But people didn't have any trouble believing Monica took her life just because she was in a flop. (An uncomfortable silence.)

DAVID. That was . . . different.

ALEX. Yes, of course it was. Forgive me. Bella's right. There are too many memories in this place. I'll help Sally change the set and we'll go on to the next scene. (He goes off L with two of the chairs. DAVID picks up his script from the floor and returns to his seat.)

DAVID (to LEO). What was that all about? What's he trying to prove? (LEO shrugs.)

LLOYD. I think . . .

(SALLY enters and takes the remaining chair off L.)

LLOYD. Talk about it later.

(ALEX returns with an awful art object on a pedestal. He places it LC in the "play within the play" area.)

ALEX. This is quite wrong, of course, but it was all I could find in the prop room. It is meant to represent an elegant art gallery.

BELLA. Another set? This play is getting expensive.

ALEX. It'll all be done in the lighting, Bella. Very imaginative and very cheap. Lloyd, will you read the scene with me?

LLOYD. Me? Why not Leo?

ALEX. I'm saving him for his own scene. Do you mind? It's . . . (He looks at his script.) . . . It's act two, page eighteen.

LLOYD (rising, opening his folder to the page, then moving to ALEX). Got it. Who do I play?

ALEX. A director.

LLOYD (reacting). More typecasting?

ALEX. It helps to give me a fix on the characters. I'll read the part of Monica again. (A beat.) Did I say Monica? Excuse me, I meant Jessica. And you'll need this . . . (He goes to his attaché case, gets a folded newspaper and brings it to LLOYD.)

LLOYD (looking at the newspaper). This paper's a year old.

ALEX. Is it? It doesn't matter. It's just a prop. (He reads from the manuscript.) The set is a Madison Avenue art gallery. (He looks at LLOYD and waves him back a few feet R.) You'll make your entrance into this scene. (LLOYD moves back a few steps. ALEX snaps his fingers and there is a blackout.) The gallery is empty. (He snaps his fingers again and the lights come up on the "play within the play" area.) Jessica wanders on . . . (ALEX moves into the light, reading from his script.) She is preoccupied, not really looking at anything . . . (He moves through the light.) She needs a few moments of solitude before the rigors of opening night. (He is now out of the light DL.) Suddenly, she thinks she has passed something she should have looked at more closely and she retraces her steps . . .

(MONICA enters the light where ALEX left it. She looks at the art object.)

She is completely unaware that someone has entered the gallery. (MONICA continues to stare at the art object, her back to the OTHERS. LLOYD steps into the light from R. He carries a few pages of the script and the prop newspaper.)

LLOYD (reading). Not my taste.

MONICA (whirling around). You startled me.

LLOYD. Next time, I'll clear my throat. (He thrusts the newspaper at MONICA.) Is this true?

MONICA. If you mean the gossip column . . .

LLOYD (no longer reading). That's exactly what I mean. Is it true?

MONICA. Yes.

LLOYD. Congratulations. Things are looking up. The actress marries the playwright and they live happily ever after . . . with him writing star vehicles for her, of course.

MONICA. That's a hostile thing to say.

LLOYD. I'm in a hostile mood. Comes from the impression that the actress had an understanding with the director.

MONICA. And what kind of understanding was that?

LLOYD. Promises of things to come. All the sidelong glances, the body language, the requests for help with your part.

MONICA. Correct me if I'm wrong, but isn't that standard procedure?

LLOYD. Not the way you did it. And it served its purpose. Special attention from the director, tender loving care.

MONICA. I think that's enough. (She turns away. LLOYD swings her back to face him.)

LLOYD. Listen to me . . . you and I really never had a go at it. Why don't we at least give it a try?

MONICA (assessing LLOYD). You're serious.

LLOYD. I could be.

MONICA. Why on earth would I tie myself down to someone like you? No talent, no money, no future. What's in it for me?

(Instead of taking offense, LLOYD becomes thoughtful. He turns away from MONICA, then suddenly calls.)

LLOYD. Lights! (The playing area blacks out. Almost immediately, full stage lights come up. ALEX is now where MONICA stood and she has exited.) You've got a major contradiction here, Alex.

ALEX. In what way?

LLOYD. Look at her character. In one scene, she's trusting and innocent, but here she's cold as ice.

ALEX. The many faces of Jessica. Besides . . . maybe that's just the way he sees her.

LLOYD. It's not clear. Did she use him or didn't she?

ALEX. The important thing is that *he* thinks she did.

DAVID. At least it's a better motive than he gave to my character.

LLOYD. I don't agree.

ALEX. All right, Lloyd, when in doubt, touch base with reality. Let's take the case of you and Monica.

LLOYD. What case?

ALEX. You were concentrating on her, giving her extra attention . . .

LLOYD. She needed it. It was her first time on stage.

ALEX. Granted. But there was talk that you were going above and beyond the call of duty.

LLOYD. That's not true.

ALEX. But suppose it was? Suppose you misinterpreted her professional needs for something more . . . personal. And then to suddenly discover that she was going to marry another man . . . (He taps the newspaper LLOYD still holds.)

LLOYD (tightly). Alex . . . what are you getting at?

ALEX. Beg pardon?

LLOYD. Are we talking about the scene or are we talking about Monica?

BELLA. Good question. (She rises and walks to ALEX and LLOYD.) Alex, we've known each other for a long time so I'm entitled to be blunt. Why are we here?

ALEX (innocently). You know why, Bella. To read my new play.

BELLA. It's not a play. It's a bunch of unrelated scenes. All of them uncomfortably close to the truth.

DAVID (rising). The hell they are! She never came to my apartment!

ALEX (going to DAVID). Who, David? Jessica or Monica?

DAVID. There isn't any Jessica. And as for Monica . . .

ALEX. Yes?

DAVID. All we had was a professional relationship.

ALEX. Just like Lloyd's?

DAVID. I don't know anything about that. I'm speaking for myself.

LLOYD (coming to DAVID and ALEX, annoyed). If you're suggesting . . .

BELLA. Darlings, darlings, darlings . . . we're all friends here.

LLOYD (looking at DAVID). I'm not so sure.

KAREN. Will somebody please tell me what's going on?

BELLA. My sentiments exactly. Alex, you owe us an explanation. If not, I've got masses of work at the office. (A beat.) Well?

ALEX. As you wish, Bella. Sit down. Finish your coffee.

BELLA (sitting). I'll sit . . . but wild horses couldn't get me to finish that coffee.

ALEX. The truth . . . if you really want it . . . is that I *am* working on a play. A murder mystery. Five suspects and an unknown killer.

LEO. Hey, I hope it's me. Makes for a better part.

KAREN. Shut up, Leo.

DAVID. My, how things change. Remember our rehearsals?

You couldn't walk behind a piece of scenery without finding them locked in an embrace.

KAREN (angrily). Time passes, David. Ingenues become leading ladies and leading men become character actors.

ALEX. Please, please . . . children, children.

KAREN. If Leo and I broke up, it's none of his business.

ALEX. But it could be mine. As a matter of fact, I have a scene about it.

KAREN (startled). You do?

BELLA. Alex, you're digressing.

ALEX. Clever of you to notice, Bella. Always business. That's what *your* scene is about, by the way. But you're right. I should come to the point. It's really very simple. When we finish here, we'll know something we didn't know before.

DAVID. And what's that?

ALEX. Which one of you killed Monica Welles. (Blackout.)

ACT TWO

SCENE: The lights come up on exactly the same moment as at the end of Act I. ALL are shocked and furious. ALEX watches them with smiling self-possession.

LLOYD. Which of us killed Monica?

KAREN. You're saying she was murdered.

LEO. And accusing one of us of doing it! The man's crazy.

DAVID. Yes. We all know you've been away, Alex. Did you go on your own or did they lock you up for a while?

ALEX. No, David. I'm quite sane.

BELLA. Then think what you're saying, Alex. Monica wasn't murdered. She committed suicide. And to suggest that one of us was involved . . .

ALEX. I didn't suggest, Bella. I made a statement of fact.

LEO. They investigated . . . the police.

ALEX. The police were wrong.

BELLA. Alex, we all know you had a terrible loss. We understand your grief. But what you're doing here . . . it won't bring Monica back . . . it won't change things.

ALEX. Then you have nothing to lose by indulging me.

KAREN (agitatedly). Nothing to lose! What have we to gain?

You bring us down here . . . make terrible accusations . . . accusations of murder and you expect us to stand here polite- ly and allow you to continue? You're a good playwright, Alex. You write good parts. But not that good! (She starts for the steps to the auditorium.)

ALEX. All I'm asking . . .

KAREN (turning to ALEX). I know what you're asking. At least I think I do. And I think you've got a helluva nerve. I'm sorry. (She continues down the steps.)

DAVID. Well, that does it. Class dismissed.

(The MAN who has been out of sight appears in the aisle and stops KAREN from leaving.)

MAN. Excuse me, Miss Daniels, but don't you think you should reconsider?

KAREN. Who are you?

MAN. We met last year after Miss Welles' suicide. I took a statement from you.

ALEX (moving to the edge of the stage). Karen . . . you remember Lieutenant McElroy.

LLOYD (walking over and peering at McELROY from the stage). McElroy. He was the investigating officer. I spoke to him myself.

DAVID. What's he doing here?

ALEX. I asked him to come. Karen, would you do me a favor and come back onstage? You, too, Lieutenant. (KAREN hesitates.)

McELROY (gently). If you wouldn't mind, ma'am. It might be helpful. (KAREN walks reluctantly back up the steps. McELROY follows her.)

BELLA (to McELROY). Perhaps you can explain all this?

McELROY. Not much to explain, ma'am. Mr. Dennison asked

me here today. He said he had new information on the death
of Monica Welles.

BELLA. A moment ago you said suicide, not death.

McELROY. Yes, ma'am. It was a suicide. That's my view and
the official determination of the medical examiner.

DAVID. Then the case is closed. Why are we wasting our time?

ALEX. Because the lieutenant is willing to give me a hearing.
That's an admirable trait, don't you think?

LLOYD. I'll tell you what's not so admirable. We didn't know
he was here.

McELROY. Mr. Dennison asked me to keep out of sight.
Thought I might inhibit you.

LEO (wryly). I wonder why.

ALEX. He agreed to intervene if any of you tried to leave.

KAREN (to McELROY). But you can't hold us here against
our will.

McELROY. No, ma'am. This is unofficial . . . you're all
perfectly free to go. But then, I'd have to wonder why you
were so anxious to leave.

BELLA. So we're back to what do we have to lose.

McELROY. Frankly, I think Mr. Dennison's on a wild goose
chase. I've told him that, but I'm willing to keep an open
mind.

ALEX. It's up to you, Karen.

KAREN (hesitating). As I said, you *do* write good parts, Alex.
Perhaps you'll forgive my little outburst and think of me the
next time you write one. (She sits.)

ALEX (smiling). Thank you. It proves again the power of the
pen. Now, I think I'll just take that objet d'art back to the
prop room and help Sally set up the next scene. (He picks
up the art object and goes off L. McELROY sits on the floor
DR at the proscenium. BELLA sits. The OTHERS look uncomfortable.)

DAVID. So we just wait. As actors always do. The puppets without the puppeteer.

KAREN. If we had any sense, we'd've all gone home.

LEO (sarcastically). And maybe lose a part for next season?

KAREN (glaring at LEO). Shut up! (To the OTHERS.) I mean, what's wrong with Alex? A year ago . . . even at the funeral . . . he was fine. But now . . .

LEO. A year is a long time. He's obsessed.

LLOYD. No. There's a method to all of this. He knows what he's doing.

DAVID. That's a charitable interpretation. He certainly raked you over the coals.

LLOYD. That makes two of us. (DAVID angrily moves DR. He fumbles in his pocket for his pipe.)

LEO (to KAREN). And we're next. Terrific.

KAREN. I don't know what he could accuse me of. Monica and I were friends.

LEO. He'll think of something.

LLOYD. If you're both so worried, read the play.

LEO. What?

LLOYD. Your scenes. They should be among the rest. Look. Forewarned is forearmed.

KAREN. Right! (She and LEO open their folders and search through the scenes.)

DAVID (to McELROY). Why are you going along with this nonsense, lieutenant?

McELROY. Is it nonsense, Mr. Mathews?

DAVID (searching in his pockets for a match). You know it is.

McELROY. The department likes to be cooperative. (He takes a lighter from his pocket and hands it to DAVID.)

DAVID. Particularly when a celebrity is involved. You're humoring him, aren't you?

McELROY. You said that, sir. I didn't.

DAVID (lighting the pipe). What's he getting at? Does he actually suspect one of us?

KAREN (rising). Nothing! No scene for us.

LLOYD. Nothing with your names on it?

LEO (hopefully). Maybe we're not going to do anything.

KAREN. After all the fuss he made about me staying?

DAVID. You won't be overlooked. Take my word for it. Your pages are probably hidden.

LEO. Why would he do that?

DAVID. Part of keeping us all off balance. He may be obsessed, Leo, but he's thorough. Very thorough. Look in his attaché case.

KAREN. Yes, let's. (She moves to the attache case DL.)

BELLA. I don't think you should.

KAREN. I don't care what you think. (She fiddles with the catch. LEO moves to her. She gets the catch open and looks in the attaché case.) It's empty!

(ALEX appears L with a small table. He slams it down in the "play within the play" area. ALL jump at the sound.)

ALEX (icily, angrily). Looking for something?

KAREN (embarassed but brazening it out). My scene. I just wanted to read it through. I hate cold readings.

ALEX. I have your pages, Karen. Here. (He taps his breast pocket.)

KAREN. Oh.

ALEX. And yours, Leo. Actually, I'd like you to play a scene together.

LEO. You mean I don't have my own scene?

KAREN. You need all the help you can get.

LEO. Isn't she wonderful? Right between the shoulder blades.

KAREN. It's easy. There's no backbone to get in the way.

ALEX (playing peacemaker). Children . . . children. (He calls off.) Sally! Would you bring me that telephone?

KAREN. Is that for our scene?

ALEX. No. I'm saving you. Giving you a big build-up. The next scene is Bella's.

BELLA (startled). Me? I'm not an actress.

LEO. At least you admit it. (KAREN glares at him.)

ALEX. Sit down, Karen . . . Leo.

(SALLY enters L with the telephone and one typed sheet of paper.)

ALEX. Put them there, please, and get set for the lights. (SALLY places the telephone and paper on the table, then exits L. He turns to BELLA.) Bella, indulge me. All producers are actresses. Just bring your chair along and sit at the table. It's just a simple phone call. Sally brought your script. (BELLA, somewhat annoyed, rises, takes her chair to the table, and sits.) The character will be a breeze for you. You're the producer of a play that's just opened to mixed notices. The after-show party is over and you're at home. The man on the other side of the line is your accountant. (He sits with KAREN, LEO and LLOYD on the arc of chairs. DAVID stands upstage of McELROY.) It's all yours, Bella. Lights! (The stage lights go out. DAVID exits R. The lights come up on the play area. BELLA picks up the telephone with one hand and holds the script with the other. She reads her scene.)

BELLA. Hello, Harry? This is . . . (She looks over to where ALEX sits in the dark.) What name shall I use?

ALEX (from the dark). Why not your own?

BELLA (after a beat of annoyance). This is Bella Lamb. Sorry to drag you out of bed but I assume you've heard about the notices . . . Yes. The patient isn't exactly terminal but the vital signs are fading fast. Harry, I know the paperwork is at your office but do you remember offhand the insurance situation? . . . No, specifically the non-appearance clause. (She looks to where ALEX sits.) I'm not sure I like this, Alex.

ALEX (from the dark). What's the problem? It's only a play.

BELLA (after a beat to control her anger). Harry, I was wondering about the amount of coverage . . . No. No particular reason. Just give me a ballpark figure. . . . Uh, huh . . . Yes, that's what I thought . . . All right, Harry. Thank you, darling. Go back to sleep. (She looks up, then over to where ALEX sits.) Satisfied? (She slams down the telephone.)

ALEX. Yes, Bella. Very realistic. You may have missed your calling. (The stage lights come up again. The play area lights go down. BELLA glares at ALEX.)

LEO. Listen, folks, I know I'm a bit slow, but I haven't the foggiest idea what that was about.

BELLA. Let me enlighten you, sweetheart. What Alex is trying to say is that I was the sole investor in *Chamber Piece*. It was all my money.

KAREN (impressed). All your money?

BELLA. Well, my husband's. What's the difference?

LEO. So?

ALEX. So Bella stood to lose a small fortune . . . and, possibly, her husband, unless —

BELLA (interrupting). Unless, like the producer in this scene, I was covered by insurance. If I kept the show open and the star failed to appear, I'd get the insurance money. Is that your drift, Alex?

ALEX (innocently). Only if you had that kind of coverage.

BELLA. It's standard. You know I did.

ALEX. Then Monica's death came at a convenient time for you.

BELLA (furious, rising and moving to ALEX). The woman

killed herself. Do you understand, Alex? Whether you want to believe it or not, she was depressed and she jumped from the terrace.

ALEX (quietly). How can you be so certain, Bella? Were you there?

LLOYD (leaping up). I get it. Alex is staging *Hamlet*.

LEO. You flipping out, Lloyd?

LLOYD. *Hamlet*, act two, scene two. The play within a play to catch his father's killer. (Quoting.) "I have heard that guilty creatures, sitting at a play, have by the very cunning of the scene, been struck so to the soul that presently they have proclaimed their malefactions . . ."

KAREN (finishing the line). "The play's the thing wherein I'll catch the conscience of the king."

BELLA. That's all very interesting, but why isn't David here? (ALL look around, startled that he is missing.)

KAREN. Do you think he went home?

ALEX. I need him here. He knows that. If he walked out . . .

LEO. What's the fuss? Maybe he went to the men's room?

BELLA (looking R). There's someone in the wings. (ALL look R.)

(DAVID appears R.)

LEO. Hey, David, they thought you bailed out.

DAVID (ignoring LEO and going to McELROY). Who are you?

McELROY. You know who I am.

DAVID. I know who you say you are. Suppose you show me some kind of identification.

BELLA. What's all this about?

DAVID. Whoever this man is, he's not Lieutenant McElroy.

LEO. What?

KAREN. But I remember him.

DAVID. You only think you do. There's a resemblance . . . same age and same build. But I'm pretty good on faces. And our friend here isn't the man who talked to me after Monica died.

BELLA. Are you sure?

DAVID. I just called the police. Lieutenant Henry McElroy was killed in the line of duty six months ago. (ALL react in astonishment. He turns to McELROY.) Now, unless you're a ghost, I think you'd better tell us who you are.

McELROY (sighing as the facade of officialdom fades away, then turning to ALEX). Well . . . I tried. (ALL turn to ALEX.)

ALEX. Ladies and gentlemen, may I introduce a fellow professional, Mr. Frank Heller.

LEO. He's an actor!

ALEX. And a very good one.

FRANK. Maybe not, Mr. Dennison. They nailed me.

ALEX. Nothing to do with your performance. Unfortunately, David has too good a memory.

BELLA (to FRANK). Are you saying that Alex hired you to impersonate Lieutenant McElroy?

FRANK. Yes, ma'am.

BELLA. But why?

ALEX. Very simple, Bella. For my little psychodrama to work, I had to keep all of you here. But given the nature of the situation, I was sure someone would try to leave. I needed . . . what shall I call it . . . official leverage.

LLOYD. Of course. We might walk out on you, but not on a cop.

ALEX. That was the idea. And since Lieutenant McElroy was no longer among the living . . .

BELLA. And since a real police officer would never cooperate . . .

ALEX. Exactly. I decided to hire a lookalike. Excuse me, David, an almost-lookalike.

DAVID. Does he know how much trouble he's in?

FRANK. What do you mean? What trouble?

DAVID. Impersonating an officer is a felony.

ALEX. *He* never said he was a police officer. *I* did.

DAVID. That's a technicality.

ALEX. If you're angry, David, blame me. Mr. Heller was just following instructions.

LEO (to FRANK). How did you get into this?

FRANK. You won't believe it, but I went to an audition.

LEO. An audition?

FRANK. My agent said that Alex Dennison was looking for an actor. Who am I to say no to that?

BELLA. Go on.

FRANK. I went to a rehearsal hall and there were maybe ten other guys. We all looked pretty much the same. Mr. Dennlson interviewed me and that was that. Then a week later he called me back. This time there were only three guys. Finally, there was just me.

BELLA. What happened when he told you what he wanted?

FRANK. I thought he was crazy.

DAVID. Accurate impression.

ALEX. Tell them the rest, Frank.

FRANK. First I said no. I mean, I never met Monica Welles but, like everybody else, I read that she committed suicide. But then he explained things to me. He told me why she was murdered and who killed her.

DAVID. Did he now?

BELLA. And, of course, he offered you money.

FRANK. Yes, ma'am.

BELLA. How much?

FRANK (looking at ALEX who nods). Ten thousand dollars.

LEO (amazed). For a one day part? For that kind of money, I'd have had plastic surgery.

FRANK. Okay, I admit the money was important. You people know how it is . . . actors have to scramble for jobs. I've tended bar. I've been a hardhat. I even drove a cab for a while. It's not much of a life. So, when this came along . . .

ALEX. You don't have to apologize, Frank.

FRANK. Anyway, no hard feelings, I hope. (To ALEX.) You won't be needing me now. I guess I should go.

ALEX. Not quite yet. No one leaves until we're finished.

DAVID. How are you going to keep us here? You don't have your phony cop anymore.

LLOYD. Right. And I've pretty much had a bellyful of this.

BELLA. We all have, Lloyd, but I think we should put up with it a few minutes longer.

DAVID (surprised). What?

BELLA. On one condition . . . that Alex tells us why he's so all-fired positive that Monica was murdered. (ALL turn to ALEX.)

KAREN. I think that's your cue, Alex.

ALEX. Frank, I'll need your help.

FRANK. What do you want me to do?

ALEX. Be Lieutenant McElroy again. We've been over this. Give them the case for suicide.

FRANK (looking around, then moving C). Well . . . there were no signs of forced entry at her apartment.

ALEX. Correct. If she was killed by an intruder, how did he get in? And why wasn't anything stolen? The police found a thousand dollars in cash on the premises. A thief would have taken it.

FRANK. She knew her play was a flop.

ALEX. So she was despondent.

FRANK. She wrote a suicide note.

ALEX. Concrete proof of her intentions.

FRANK. After everybody left, she went into her bedroom, out

on her terrace and she . . . she . . .

ALEX. Say it.

FRANK. She jumped.

ALEX. In the words of the medical examiner's report, "Fall from a height." Case closed.

LLOYD. But not for you.

ALEX (flaring). Nobody commits suicide because of bad reviews.

LLOYD. It wasn't the reviews. It was the end of a dream for her.

KAREN. Alex, you have to admit that sometimes she was . . . well, erratic. I mean, she walked out before a performance one night. I had to go on for her. Don't you remember?

ALEX. Yes, the police made quite a point of that. Monica Welles gets into an argument with the playwright just before a preview. She bolts from the theatre, hails a cab, and goes home. She refuses to answer her phone, so we're forced to give a performance without her. She comes to the theatre a few hours later and apologizes. Obviously proof of an unsound mind.

DAVID. It's certain proof of something.

ALEX. David, she was in love. She was struggling over whether or not to make a commitment. The tension was too much for her. We fought, she ran out, she came back. It was unprofessional . . . she admitted that . . . but it wasn't abnormal.

BELLA. I've been listening very carefully, Alex, but I'm not hearing any evidence of murder.

ALEX. She called me that night. She asked me to come over. Is that the behavior of a suicide?

BELLA. Maybe it was a cry for help.

ALEX. Then why did the line go dead in the middle of a sentence?

BELLA. Because she changed her mind and hung up. The

woman was under stress. She wasn't rational.

ALEX. She was rational enough to make herself a pot of tea. I saw it on a table in the study.

DAVID. That's your evidence? A pot of tea?

ALEX (agitatedly). She was starting a new life. She had everything to live for. You saw her at the party. Was that a woman in despair?

KAREN. Nobody can get into someone else's mind, Alex. Not even people we care about. Who knows what she was thinking that night?

ALEX. I know. She was thinking about our future.

BELLA (moving to ALEX and embracing him sympathetically). Alex . . . Alex, don't you see? Monica did a terrible thing. She not only took her own life, but she rejected you. That's hard to accept. So you've come up with this fantasy about a murder. In a strange way, it's easier for you to live with.

ALEX (coldly). I take it that means you're not going to help.

BELLA. I just don't see what else we can do.

ALEX (breaking away from BELLA, speaking more agitatedly). Karen, Leo . . . will you play the last scene for me?

KAREN. Alex, Bella's right. We're all your friends but we're not getting anywhere with this.

ALEX. Leo? It's just a few pages.

LEO (embarrassed). I'm sorry. (After an uncomfortable silence, KAREN picks up her purse.)

DAVID. Does anyone want to share a ride uptown?

LLOYD. Sure. You can drop me at seventy-fifth street. (ALL, including FRANK, get ready to leave and move toward the steps down from the stage. ALEX looks desperate, then calls.)

ALEX (standing DR). Just a moment. (ALL pause L near the steps, then turn to him. He pulls out a gun and holds it on them.)

DAVID (astonished). What the hell . . .

BELLA. Alex, for God's sake . . .

ALEX. Come back here, please.

BELLA. All right. Fine. But you don't need that.

ALEX. It seems I do.

DAVID. Give me that thing before somebody gets hurt. (He moves to ALEX who points the gun at him.)

KAREN. David, don't.

DAVID (hesitating). He's bluffing.

LLOYD. I wouldn't count on it.

LEO (laughing uneasily). Hey, Alex, that's just a prop, right? It's not loaded.

ALEX. Don't try to find out, Leo. Now, I'm sorry but I'll have to ask you all to move very slowly to the center of the stage where I can see you . . . very slowly. (ALL begin to move C.)

(A huge, burly MAN appears from the wings R behind ALEX.)

MAN. Which of you is Alex Dennison? (KAREN and BELLA cry out slightly. DAVID tries to indicate to the MAN that ALEX has a gun. ALEX holds the gun down, out of sight.)

ALEX (without turning). I am. And you are?

MAN. Santoro. Santoro Moving and Storage. Gotcha shipment.

ALEX (calling). Sally . . . Where's your truck, Mr. Santoro?

SANTORO. By the stage door. Want me to unload?

(SALLY appears L.)

ALEX. Sally, will you close the traveler, then go show Mr. Santoro where to put the things.

SALLY. How do I close it?

ALEX. There's a rope on the wall, dear. Just pull it. (SALLY exits L.) Santoro, you can start unloading. Miss Bean will show you where everything goes.

SANTORO. You got it.

KAREN (just as SANTORO turns to go). Wait a minute. (ALEX points the gun at her.)

SANTORO. Yeah?

KAREN. Nothing.

SANTORO (thinking they're all crazy). Actresses! (He turns back and goes off R, calling.) Okay, guys, dump it.

ALEX (pointing at the table in the "play within the play" area with the gun). Lloyd, will you move that table center? And David, bring a few of the chairs downstage. Quickly, please. Help David, Frank. (ALL do as they are told.) Leo, you and Karen come get your scene. (LEO and KAREN approach ALEX.)

KAREN. You expect us to act?

ALEX. That's exactly what I expect. (He fumbles in his pocket for the scene. The furniture has now been moved downstage and the traveler closes.)

SALLY (from offstage L). Did I get the right rope?

ALEX. Perfect. Come here now, please. (He takes the pages from his pocket and gives them to KAREN and LEO.)

(SALLY enters L below the curtain, near BELLA.)

BELLA (to SALLY, trying not to be heard). Alex has a gun.

SALLY. Really? Gee, show business is exciting. (She goes over to ALEX.) Yes, Mr. Dennison?

ALEX (handing SALLY another piece of paper). Here's a floor plan. Make sure the moving men follow it exactly.

SALLY. Right. (She exits R.)

ALEX. Everyone ready?

BELLA. Alex, we'll cooperate . . . just put that away.

ALEX. All right. In the interest of calming your nerves. But

I'll keep it handy. (He puts the gun in his jacket pocket.) Karen, the scene takes place in your dressing room. It's opening night. That's your dressing table. (He indicates the table LLOYD moved C.) Leo, you make your entrance in a few moments. Ready?

KAREN. No.

ALEX. But you'll try, won't you? (He pats the gun in his pocket.) Sit at the table. I don't think we'll bother with lights for this scene. (He goes to the center of the traveler and looks around. FRANK sits on the floor at the proscenium L. BELLA sits on a chair beside FRANK. DAVID stands behind BELLA. LLOYD sits R. LEO stands beside him, waiting for his cue.) Again, I'll read Monica's part. The scene starts with a knock on the door. (He raps his heel on the floor to simulate a knock.)

KAREN (reading). Yes?

ALEX (reading). It's Monica. (He slips through the fold of the curtain.)

KAREN (reading, surprised). Monica?

ALEX (from behind the curtain). Yes. May I come in?

MONICA (from behind the curtain, echoing ALEX). May I come in?

KAREN (reading). Yes, of course.

(MONICA comes through the center of the curtain dressed in the dressing gown from the first scene.)

MONICA. Not in makeup yet?

KAREN (no longer reading). Oh, I won't put it on for another hour. I just want to sit here and soak up the atmosphere.

MONICA. And you're not quite sure which makeup to use, are you?

KAREN. Pardon?

MONICA. I mean, if I got sick at the last minute, you'd have to play my part.

KAREN. Never even crossed my mind. Nobody gets sick opening night.

MONICA. No, I suppose not. You were quite good when you went on for me last week.

KAREN (shrugging). The audience was disappointed. I did my best, but there's no comparison.

MONICA. You're being modest.

KAREN. It doesn't much matter, does it? I mean, you're here.

MONICA. That seems to surprise you.

KAREN (carefully). Why would I be surprised?

MONICA (removing a small, decorated tea cannister from the folds of her robe and setting it on the dressing table). I brought your tea back. (KAREN looks uneasy.) You remember. The special blend of tea your grandmother whips up in her country kitchen.

KAREN. Didn't you like it? It really calms me down.

MONICA. So you said. Have some before opening night. Wonderful for the nerves.

KAREN. It is.

MONICA. Maybe. But not so good for the rest of the body.

KAREN (guardedly). I don't know what you mean.

MONICA. Then let me see if I can make myself clear. After you practically forced the tea on me, and since your motives are somewhat transparent, I took it to my doctor and asked him to send a sample to a lab.

KAREN. A . . . lab?

MONICA. I learned a marvelous new word. Cyclophosfamide. It's an alkylating agent. Odd thing to find in your grandmother's recipe.

KAREN. There must be some mistake.

MONICA. It causes dizziness and nausea. A few sips and I'd be home right now. And you'd know which makeup to use.

KAREN. Monica . . .

MONICA. You weren't even willing to pay your dues, were you?

LEO (rushing into the scene, angling himself as though he came through the curtain). Karen . . . I . . . oops! Didn't know you had company. Hi, Monica.

KAREN (tightly). This is private, Leo.

MONICA. Not at all. Stay, Leo. The three of us should have a talk.

LEO (bewildered and looking from one to the other). About what?

MONICA. Pick a subject. Opening nights. Helping your wife's career.

LEO. Huh?

MONICA. Or should we talk about medical school? You *did* go to one for a few years, didn't you? I imagine you took courses in chemistry.

LEO. Hey, that was a long time ago. Why? (He turns to KAREN, worried.) What's this all about?

KAREN. She knows.

LEO. Knows what? (Agitated, KAREN picks up the tea cannister and slams it down again.)

KAREN. About this. She had it analyzed.

LEO (like a body blow). Oh, brother . . .

KAREN. All right, we spiked your tea. It wouldn't have harmed you, just . . . slowed you down for tonight. The question is, what are you going to do?

LEO. I told you it was crazy. You wouldn't listen.

KAREN. Be quiet!

LEO. They put people in jail for something like this.

(SANTORO appears DR.)

SANTORO.   Excuse me, Mr. Dennison, we're finished.   (ALL look at him. MONICA slips through the curtain.)

(ALEX comes through the curtain to replace MONICA.)

SANTORO.   We'll be back in the morning to get the stuff.

ALEX.   Fine. Thank you. (SANTORO exits DR.) Shall we see the set for the last scene?

BELLA (impatiently). Another scene?

KAREN.   Alex, I hope you know that scene we just played is nothing but lies.

ALEX.   You did bring her tea. She told me.

KAREN.   It was a gift and there was nothing in it. I mean, what good would it do me? Bella would never open with an understudy.

ALEX.   Would you, Bella? Or would you send everybody home at the last minute? Critics, the press . . . I wonder.

LEO.   Alex, use your head. Even if Karen was nuts, I'm not. I'd never help her with something like that.

ALEX.   You were trying to save your marriage. You'd have done anything she wanted.

LEO.   No way.

BELLA.   Alex, if there is another scene, let's look at the set and get it over with.

ALEX.   The voice of reason.

DAVID.   At least one of us is rational.

ALEX.   Just strike this table, David, please. (DAVID moves the table off L.)

(SALLY appears in the curtain.)

ALEX.   Get ready on the curtain, Sally.

SALLY (taking the chair off L). Looks like a real show. (The

OTHERS draw to the sides of the stage.)

ALEX. Everybody ready?

ALL. Yes!

ALEX. Sally! (The curtain opens on Monica's study, exactly as it was before.)

KAREN. Oh, Lord! That's Monica's apartment!

ALEX. Very good, Karen. Her study. The scene of the crime.

KAREN. But how?

ALEX. Her furniture was in storage. I had it brought here today . . . in the interest of realism. (He calls off.) Lights, Sally. (The set is gradually lit. The downstage lights dim out. The OTHERS move around the set.)

DAVID (at the desk, reading the paper in the typewriter). "I'm sorry, but it's better . . ." (He realizes what he's reading and breaks off.) Is this . . .?

ALEX. The original? No. The police have it in their files. Everything is exactly as it was . . . the tray of liquor, the pot of tea . . . (On small table between sofa and chair.) . . . the contents of the drawer. Even our champagne glasses. (The glasses are on the table UC. DAVID takes out his pipe.) I wouldn't, David. Monica didn't smoke. There are no ash trays. (DAVID puts the pipe away. To KAREN by the chair L which is set incorrectly.) Karen, that chair is out of position. Move it stage right, will you? (KAREN tries to lift the chair but it is too heavy. LEO crosses to her and moves it to its proper place. FRANK stands DR, watching with interest.)

BELLA. Well, what now?

ALEX. Alibis, Bella.

BELLA. I was wondering when you'd get around to that.

ALEX. I've established that you all had motives.

DAVID. The hell you have.

ALEX. But motives are nullified by a legitimate alibi.

DAVID. Then cross me off your list. I didn't want to go home.

I went to an after-hours club. I was there till four in the morning. I must have twenty witnesses.

LLOYD. And I was with my agents. We went back to my place after the party and commiserated.

ALEX. Bella?

BELLA. My husband and I took Meg Jones, the columnist, home. She asked us up and we talked for hours. I thought it might get us a mention in the column and I knew we needed all the publicity we could get.

ALEX. Karen, that leaves you and Leo.

KAREN. Easy. As you keep reminding us, we were married then. We went home to bed.

BELLA. Seems like everyone's accounted for.

ALEX. Then who was Monica planning to meet after the party? (ALL look at each other in surprise.)

LLOYD. Who says she was meeting anybody?

ALEX. She sent me home, Lloyd . . . on the one night I should have stayed. She also got rid of the caterers. Didn't even give them a chance to clean up. No, she was expecting someone.

DAVID. You're saying she didn't want you there because someone was coming?

ALEX. It explains the circumstances, doesn't it? After I left, she let him in.

KAREN. Him?

ALEX. Or her. They had some kind of argument. She called me. He grabbed the phone and hung up. I think there was a struggle. She was struck and killed.

BELLA. Where did all this happen?

ALEX. Right here in the study.

BELLA. Why not in the bedroom? Or the living room?

ALEX. The tea, Bella. She brought it in here. (He points to the tea.)

DAVID. We're back to that again. Maybe she forgot. She was upset.

ALEX. Won't wash, David. Not too upset to *make* a pot of tea but too upset to drink it? Then, of course, she didn't turn off the lights. They were all on when the police came in. And the bedroom door was open.

DAVID. Meaning?

ALEX. Suicide is a private act. She'd called me. I might come and stop her. She knew I had a key. So first, chain the door. And, secondly, close and lock the bedroom door. But she didn't. After the party, she was never in the bedroom alive.

DAVID. So your imaginary murderer carries her on to the terrace and throws her off?

ALEX. Why not? Instead of an unexplained corpse, he creates a suicide.

BELLA. And the note?

ALEX (going to the desk and opening the top-right drawer). He searches. Finds a piece of her stationery in here.

KAREN. What about fingerprints?

ALEX. Gloves. Handkerchief? (Using his pocket handkerchief, he takes a piece of paper from the drawer, then closes it.) He presses this to her fingers, then rolls it in the typewriter. Her prints are on it. His aren't.

BELLA. Very ingenious, Alex. But even if you're right . . . even if somebody did kill her . . . it wasn't one of us. Unless you don't believe our alibis.

ALEX. On the contrary, I hired a firm of private detectives to check them out. And most of them held up.

DAVID. Most of them?

ALEX. Three of you were with witnesses when Monica died. David, you were at the club. Lloyd, you were with your agents and Bella, you were with Meg Jones.

LEO. Now, hold on!

ALEX. But you and Karen, Leo . . . you two only alibi each other.

KAREN. We were together!

ALEX. But we have only your word for that.

BELLA. What are you saying?

ALEX. There are five motives here, all hypothetical. But one of them is real. It's a matter of record. (He takes a paper from his attaché case and gives it to BELLA.) Read it.

BELLA (scanning the paper). This is a laboratory report. Chemical analysis of a tea sample submitted by Monica Welles in April of last year.

LLOYD. What does it say?

BELLA. The sample was saturated with . . . I can't even pronounce it . . . but it can cause illness and incapacitation. (She lowers the paper. ALL look at LEO and KAREN.)

ALEX. I found that among her effects.

LEO. It's a fake!

BELLA. Looks genuine to me, Leo. Easy enough to check.

ALEX. One legitimate motive . . . two unsupported alibis.

KAREN. I'm not going to listen to this.

ALEX. She found out what you were doing. Both of you pleaded with her. You asked to see her after the party.

KAREN. No!

ALEX. You're the lady who would stick pins in a photograph to get a part . . . and you were Monica's understudy.

KAREN. I never went back there!

ALEX. Then who did?

KAREN. I don't know. Maybe Leo . . .

ALEX. But you were *with* Leo!

KAREN. Not all the time. He . . . went out for a while.

ALEX. That's what I wanted to hear.

LEO (to KAREN). What are you doing to me?

KAREN. Well, you did! You said you couldn't sleep. You wanted to take a walk.

ALEX. How long was he gone, Karen?

KAREN. I . . . don't remember. Twenty minutes . . . an hour.

ALEX. No alibi, Leo . . . and a motive!

LEO. Hey, this is crazy! Don't tell me any of you believes this? All right. I took a walk. Is that some kind of crime! (He turns to KAREN, angrily.) And what about her? If I don't have an alibi, neither does she.

ALEX. It doesn't matter, Leo.

LEO. Why the hell doesn't it?

ALEX. Because Monica was killed in here. The murderer had to carry her out onto the terrace, lift her over the rail. And, as you all saw, Karen couldn't even move that chair. (LEO takes a step or two toward the steps. ALEX, coldly furious, pulls out his gun.) You killed her, Leo.

LEO. She killed herself! I'm getting out of here. (He starts down the steps.)

ALEX. Her whole life ahead of her and you killed her!

BELLA. Alex, take it easy.

ALEX. Come back here, Leo.

LEO. You're not going to hang this on me.

ALEX. I'm warning you . . .

DAVID. Leo, listen to him.

LEO. I've done enough listening. (He starts up the aisle. ALEX rushes to the edge of the stage and aims his gun.)

KAREN. Alex, no! (ALEX fires. KAREN screams.)

DAVID. Good God! (LEO tries to run, trips and sprawls in the aisle. LLOYD and DAVID move toward ALEX. Angry, he turns and points the gun at them. BELLA, DL, turns and runs off. LLOYD and DAVID back off. ALEX walks to the steps and points the gun at LEO in the aisle.)

LEO. No! Please . . . (ALEX cocks the trigger.)

KAREN. Somebody *do* something! (A blackout. There is another shot and shouting. ALL are confused and the voices overlap in the dark.)

DAVID. Get Alex!

LLOYD. Where is he?

BELLA. Over there . . . near the steps.

KAREN. Leo, are you all right? (There are sounds of a scuffle. ALL ad lib words in struggle.)

DAVID. I've got him.

BELLA. Careful of the gun.

DAVID. Lloyd, give me a hand. (There is another shot. BELLA screams.)

KAREN. Somebody turn on the lights!

SALLY. I can't. She must've pulled the master switch. I don't know where it is.

LLOYD. What did you do, Bella?

BELLA. I don't know.

KAREN. Please, aren't there any lights in here? (Suddenly the beam of a flashlight cuts through the darkness, searching for ALEX.)

FRANK. I've got a flashlight. Where is he? (There is total silence.) Somebody say something! Tell me where he is! (The circle of the flashlight roams the stage. It picks out LLOYD, standing quietly, then KAREN, expressionless. Then it finds DAVID, immobile. Finally, it picks out ALEX, the gun by his side. He is calm, even casual.)

ALEX. Lights, Sally. (There is a pause, then the full stage lights come on blindingly bright. FRANK stands by the desk. The drawer is open. He looks at the OTHERS who stand quietly, looking at him. He tries to understand what's happened.)

(SALLY and BELLA enter L. LEO calmly walks up from the aisle.)

FRANK. What is this? What's going on?

ALEX. Where did you get the flashlight, Frank?

FRANK (bewildered). What?

ALEX. The flashlight. Where did you get it?

FRANK. Right here. In the drawer.

ALEX. How did you know it was there?

FRANK. I didn't. I was just . . . looking. You know . . . for matches.

ALEX. Monica didn't smoke. I made that clear. Why would she have matches in her desk?

FRANK. What the hell *is* this?

ALEX. Why did you open that particular drawer?

FRANK. It was dark. I opened a lot of drawers.

ALEX. No, you didn't. Try them. (A pause. FRANK tugs at the other drawers which will not open.) I had all the drawers sealed. All except one. And that's the one you opened.

FRANK. So what? What difference does it make?

ALEX. You went to that drawer because you knew you'd find a flashlight.

FRANK (to the OTHERS). What's he talking about? (To ALEX.) How would I know that?

ALEX. Because you saw it the night you killed Monica . . . when you took out a piece of stationery for her suicide note.

FRANK (indicating LEO). He could have seen it. He was there. You said so yourself.

LEO. He doesn't get it yet.

FRANK. Get what?

BELLA. Leo wasn't there at all. After the party, he went home to his wife and three children.

FRANK (stunned). What?

DAVID. And the closest he ever got to medical school was playing a male nurse off-Broadway.

LEO. I was very good in that.

FRANK. But . . . he said . . .

BELLA. We all said a lot of things. None of them were true.

FRANK. You had motives.

LLOYD. Afraid not.

FRANK (to KAREN). You wanted her out of the way.

KAREN. You mean Grandma's homemade tea? No such concoction. It was just part of the script.

FRANK. Script?

ALEX. Listen carefully, Frank. Nothing here today was real. Nothing. The scenes we played, the arguments . . . they all came out of my typewriter. With a little improvisation from my friends.

LEO. I thought we were terrific.

FRANK. This is crazy . . .

ALEX. As for the motives, we invented them. Karen and Leo were never married. At least, not to each other.

KAREN (grinning). How is your wife, Leo?

LEO (smiling and nodding). Pregnant again.

ALEX. David and Monica were close friends. Her relationship with Lloyd was strictly professional.

BELLA. And I *never* put my own money in a play. And certainly not my husband's. He'd kill me.

DAVID. Oh, almost forgot. (He reaches into his pocket.) Here's your lighter back.

FRANK. You kept it.

ALEX. Wouldn't do for you to have a lighter in your pocket, Frank. You might not have gone for the flashlight.

FRANK (beginning to understand). Then this whole thing was staged.

ALEX. For an audience of one.

FRANK (walking to ALEX and pointing to the gun). Blanks? (ALEX nods.) And the auditions? Hiring me to play a cop?

ALEX. Just an excuse to get you here. We had to make you a participant. We even recreated her study so you'd be back where you were a year ago.

BELLA. And then we agreed I'd pull the lights . . .

FRANK (sinking into a chair). How did you know about me and Monica? (This is tantamount to a confession. The OTHERS relax. During the following conversation, each of them casually drifts out of the study set. BELLA, SALLY and LLOYD go DL. DAVID, KAREN and LEO go DR.)

ALEX. I didn't at first. But it was obvious she was expecting someone that night.

FRANK. But why me? Out of all the people in New York.

ALEX. Earlier that evening, she asked if I could stop someone from working. I thought it was a strange thing to say. And later, she was counting money . . . a thousand dollars.

FRANK. So?

ALEX. It suddenly occurred to me that it might be blackmail money. Maybe she was paying someone off.

FRANK. That still doesn't explain . . .

ALEX. A thousand isn't much. Who would she think she could buy for that kind of money? And who could Alex Dennison, a successful playwright, keep from working?

LEO. An actor, naturally.

ALEX. If there *was* a blackmailer, and he was coming for a pay-off, he'd probably wait outside till our party was over. And it was raining that night.

DAVID. Alex remembered there was a cab parked across the street with an off-duty sign. I was complaining about it.

ALEX. I also remembered the day Monica ran out of here during previews. She took a cab home.

LEO. And we all know the cliché about out-of-work actors driving taxis.

KAREN. In fact, Mr. Heller, you did say you drove one yourself for a while.

ALEX. Every cab company keeps records of pick-ups and deliveries. It seems that a Frank Heller took a fare from this theatre to Monica's address the afternoon of our fight. He also had his cab out the night of the murder . . . with no recorded fares. (ALEX and FRANK are now alone in the study set.)

FRANK. Why didn't you go to the police?

ALEX. With what? Suspicions? No, we had to prove you were in her apartment that night. And since we're all creatures of the theatre . . .

FRANK. Yeah. You decided to do a number on me. You were good. You were all good.

ALEX. What happened that night, Frank? (He leaves the study.)

FRANK. That's right. Without me, you don't have a second act finish, do you? (The stage lights dim out. FRANK is caught in a spotlight.) I was parked across the street waiting for all of you to leave. The party broke up early . . . some of the guests even tried to get me to take them somewhere in the rain. I was pretty tense. I'd had a few drinks and just sitting there was driving me crazy. Finally, she sent the caterers home and I went up . . . (A door chime rings.) . . . She was expecting me. She opened the door. She was carrying a tray with tea things . . . (He rises, in the scene now.) . . . Hi, Monica.

MONICA (from offstage, brusquely). Go into the study.

FRANK. Not even a hello, Monica?

MONICA (from offstage, curtly). Through that door. (The lights come up on the study set. FRANK stands at the center of the set, looking uncomfortable.)

(MONICA is setting the tea tray on the table next to the sofa.)

FRANK. How were the reviews?

MONICA. You don't give a damn about the reviews.

FRANK. Okay. No polite conversation. You want to get down to business, we'll get down to business. But you were a lot friendlier the last time I was here.

MONICA. This isn't the last time. Frank, I want you to understand something. I was angry at Alex. He opened up some emotions I didn't know I had and, like a fool, I guess I wanted to punish him for it. So when I got in your cab that day . . .

FRANK. I couldn't believe it. Monica Welles coming on to me . . . inviting me up for a drink.

MONICA. I was using you . . . or, at least, in a crazy moment I planned to. Some nutty idea of making Alex jealous. But I came to my senses and I asked you to leave. Nothing happened.

FRANK. But he doesn't know that. We were together for hours. You even missed a performance.

MONICA. Do you really think he'll believe I picked up a cab driver and let him make love to me?

FRANK. Maybe. Maybe not. But I'm betting you'd rather pay a few bucks and forget the whole thing.

MONICA. Nuisance value.

FRANK. Call it whatever you like. Look, I don't enjoy doing this. But what do I have going for me? I've been an actor for fifteen years and I'm driving a cab. I need a stake, something to get me moving again. So, when I opened the paper this morning . . .

MONICA. You saw Alex and I were getting married.

FRANK. I figured he was a lucky man. Why shouldn't I be lucky, too?

MONICA. Frank, I got you into this, so I owe you something. If you walk away now, I'll never mention your name to anyone.

FRANK. Sorry. (MONICA realizes she won't be able to move him. She suddenly moves decisively to the desk and picks up the telephone.) What are you doing?

MONICA. I was going to pay you. I actually went to the bank and took out a thousand dollars.

FRANK. We were talking about a lot more than that.

MONICA. Doesn't matter, Frank. Because you're not getting

anything.

FRANK. Oh?

MONICA. Tonight I decided that even if you called it off, I'd still tell Alex the truth.

FRANK. Not very smart. Especially right before the wedding.

MONICA. It's about time I was honest with him. (She dials.) As you said, maybe he'll forgive me, maybe he won't. Either way, he's not going to forgive a blackmailer.

FRANK. Now wait.

MONICA. I wouldn't want to be you, Frank. He has a lot of friends. (Into the phone.) Alex? I know how awful it is out but can you possibly come back here? . . . Right now. Alex, I'm sorry, but . . . please. It's terribly important . . . I did, but . . . (FRANK, frightened, crosses the room, pulls the phone away from MONICA, and hangs it up.)

FRANK. Do you know what you're doing?

MONICA. I think so.

FRANK. You're going to ruin things for yourself.

MONICA. Why don't we wait and see? You're welcome to stay, Frank. I'm sure he'll want to meet you. (The phone rings.)

FRANK. Don't answer it! (MONICA ignores him and reaches for the phone from the upstage side of the desk. He runs to her.) I said, don't answer it! (He grabs Monica's shoulders, shakes her and, using more force than he intends, hurls her to the floor behind the desk. We hear a loud thump. He yells.) *Monica*! Monica? (He backs away a step or two. Monica's hand falls limply into view from behind the desk. The phone continues to ring. The study lights go down and the spotlight picks up FRANK. When the study is dark, the phone ceases to ring and FRANK speaks. He moves downstage. MONICA exits in the darkness.) I called her name . . . I tried to revive her. I even took her pulse. I could feel it flickering for a few seconds . . . then it stopped. When I realized that she was dead, I didn't know what to do.

ALEX (from the dark). So you manufactured a suicide.

FRANK. I didn't want a murder investigation. I cleaned away her blood from the corner of the desk. I carried her into the bedroom . . . and you know the rest. (A beat.) Look, I've been living with this for a long time. I did what I did. But it was an accident. For whatever it's worth, I didn't mean to kill her. (He sits again in the chair where he was when the scene began. The spotlight dims out and full stage lights come up. ALEX walks downstage and calls into the auditorium.)

ALEX. You up in the light booth, Loretta?

LORETTA (from the back of the auditorium). Here, Alex.

ALEX (calling). Is the lieutenant with you?

LORETTA. He's on his way down.

(The LIEUTENANT, a gray-haired man of fifty in a rumpled suit, appears in the aisle.)

LIEUTENANT. Here I am, Mr. Dennison.

ALEX. You heard?

LIEUTENANT. From the very beginning.

FRANK. Who's that?

ALEX. Frank, meet the man you impersonated . . . Lieutenant McElroy.

FRANK. But you said he was . . .

DAVID. Killed in the line of duty. I believe that was the dialogue. Delivered, as always, with my well-known credibility. (The LIEUTENANT comes up on the stage.)

ALEX. Thanks for coming, Lieutenant.

LIEUTENANT. Good thing I did. Looks like I owe you an apology.

ALEX. Not really. I didn't have any proof.

LIEUTENANT. Consider me a convert. You've done our work

for us.

FRANK (to ALEX). I don't look like him at all.

ALEX. I had to give you a reason for being here, Frank . . . one that you'd believe.

LIEUTENANT. Come along, Mr. Heller. (He takes Frank's arm. They start to the steps. FRANK pauses and looks back at ALEX.)

FRANK. If you ever write a play about this . . . at least I gave you an ending. (He and the LIEUTENANT exit up the aisle. The OTHERS gather around ALEX. KAREN hugs ALEX.)

ALEX. Thank you . . . all of you.

DAVID. I never thought it would work.

BELLA. Especially with me. I kept worrying I'd blow my lines.

KAREN. I hate to admit it, Bella, but you weren't half-bad. I mean for a non-pro.

LLOYD. You know, the one thing I don't understand is why he went along with it.

ALEX. Frank Heller?

LLOYD (nodding). You promised him a lot of money and you told him it was a trap for Leo. That made him feel safe. You'd pin it on the wrong man and stop looking. But even so, *he* knew he killed Monica. Why get involved at all?

ALEX. For one reason, Lloyd. He's an actor. I was offering him a wonderful part.

BELLA. Darlings, it's over. It's all been too exhausting. I think we all deserve to go down the street to Nora's and have some of her revolting coffee.

LEO. Who's paying?

BELLA. It's the producer who always pays! (She goes down the steps and out through the back of the auditorium. The OTHERS follow.)

KAREN (last, at the top of the steps). Alex?

ALEX. Save me a place. (KAREN blows him a kiss, runs down

the steps and up the aisle.   ALEX goes DR, reaches off, and
pulls the work light back on to where it was at the opening. He
moves back into the study set and picks one of the champagne
glasses up from the table UC. He clinks it against the other in a
silent toast and sips, then walks off L. Simultaneously, the
stage lights go out and the work light goes on.)

CURTAIN

The study is in Alex's memory so while the furniture is real, the set need not be realistic. Lighting may define the area rather than real walls.

There is a window unit R, marking the wall. A desk is set perpendicular to the window. The desk chair is downstage so that anyone seated in it will face away from the audience. A phone, lamp and typewriter are on the desk. There are several drawers visible to the audience. At center, angled slightly left, is a small sofa. A chair is at right angles to the upstage end of the sofa. There is a small table between them.

A door unit UR leads to the bedroom, another UL faces L and leads to the living room. A bar or table with drinks defines the back wall UC.

DIRECTOR'S NOTES

DIRECTOR'S NOTES

DIRECTOR'S NOTES

DIRECTOR'S NOTES

DIRECTOR'S NOTES

DIRECTOR'S NOTES